BUDGET TRAVEL THROUGH SPACE AND TIME

Albert Goldbarth

Graywolf Press

SAINT PAUL, MINNESOTA

Publication of this volume is made possible in part by a grant provided by the Minnesota State Arts Board, through an appropriation by the Minnesota State Legislature; a grant from the Wells Fargo Foundation Minnesota; and a grant from the National Endowment for the Arts, which believes that a great nation deserves great art. Significant support has also been provided by the Bush Foundation; Target and Mervyn's with support from the Target Foundation; the McKnight Foundation; and other generous contributions from foundations, corporations, and individuals. To these organizations and individuals we offer our heartfelt thanks.

MINNESOTA
STATE ARTS BOARD

NATIONAL
ENDOWMENT
FOR THE ARTS

Published by Graywolf Press
2402 University Avenue, Suite 203
Saint Paul, Minnesota 55114
All rights reserved.

www.graywolfpress.org

Published in the United States of America
Printed in Canada

ISBN 1-55597-416-3

2 4 6 8 9 7 5 3 1
First Graywolf Printing, 2005

Library of Congress Control Number: 2004109268

Cover design: Kyle G. Hunter

Cover art: *A Voyage to Cacklogallinia* (1727)
Used with permission from the Ordway Collection at the U.S. Space & Rocket Center,
Huntsville, Alabama

Budget Travel through Space and Time

Other Books by Albert Goldbarth

ACKNOWLEDGMENTS

My gratitude to the editors of the following, who found space and time for these poems:

American Letters and Commentary: Hoverers
Another Chicago Magazine: The Initial Published Discovery
Antioch Review: #1117
Beloit Poetry Journal: Heart Heart Heart Heart Heart Heart Heart; 27,000 Miles; Vacation: Carolina Coast; Patoot and Poopik; Geese Jazz; Poet-Spouse Observer-Thoughts
Black Warrior Review: A Knife through the Head (Your Distresses and Mine)
Boulevard: Some Ways; Lucky's Story; Time in the Victorian Novel; Problemata Aristotelis
Georgia Review: "You Might Notice Blood in Your Urine for a Couple of Weeks" / & Scenes from the American Revolution
Gettysburg Review: Budget Travel through the Universe; Waters
Iowa Review: Where the Membrane Is Thinnest
Kenyon Review: Ötzi; The Feelers; Five Pounds; The Spices
Laurel Review: A Gesture Made in the Martian Wastes
Mid-American Review: The Views
New Letters: The Rocket Ship
Nightsun: The Two Directions
Ohio Review: Called from Out of the Lines of Your Life
Ontario Review: Scenes from the Next Life
Parnassus: Into That Story
Poetry: The Invisible World; Some Common Terms in Latin That Are Larger Than Our Lives; Swan; Washington's Ovens, Adamses' Letters
Prairie Schooner: The Sign
Quarterly West: Thread
River Styx: Tuvalu
Salt Hill: About the Dead
Shenandoah: Branches
Southwest Review: "Far": An Etymology

Virginia Quarterly Review: Scale-Model Sketch
Willow Springs: Three Days: Three Sections

"Heart Heart Heart Heart Heart Heart Heart," "'You Might Notice Blood in Your Urine
for a Couple of Weeks' / & Scenes from the American Revolution," and "The Spices"
were recycled on the *Poetry Daily* Web site; "27,000 Miles" was reprinted in *Birds in the
Hand* (North Point Press).

No computer was used in the creation and submission of these poems, and I want to provide
additional thanks to the editors above for their generosity in the production process.

CONTENTS

. . . from everlasting to everlasting . . .

EDMOND HAMILTON

Space and Time

Budget Travel through the Universe ⁓

We can rig a supernova in a single laptop jiffy.
Ditto werewolf transformation: every feral hair
is given its credible gumption and its little jacket of oil.
As for aliens summoned from out of the holes
in space itself . . . we're crackerjack on aliens,
a seven-story studio exists to make their travel
to our planet a persuasive thing. And yet, today
at a festival of silent film, I'm moved by what was possible
in 1910: a city street is empty;
then the camera stops; a man's positioned standing in that street;
and then the camera rolls again. It could be a man from the moon
has suddenly appeared on our world, without even the help
of a pair of blunt-tip sewing-basket scissors.

⁓

"The fastest and the vastest"—some
loud-trumpeted ad slogan a while ago, for yet another
überglobal, multizillion-dollar, telecyberfiber transport system:
microchips and oil tankers in a great dance of delivery,
eight-ton robot arm and transatlantic corridor and satellite bounce.
But it can be more modest, and can still arrive
on time and with adequate flash. "The fact is, shooting stars
are between the size of a grain of rice and a grain of sand."
And everybody's consequential journey
through the fallopian tube.

⁓

The dreams came. She was looking at herself
in the small mirror that hung above the washstand,
and the face that gazed back from the glass was the wondering
unmarked face of a child (Paula Volsky,
The Grand Ellipse).
                    Is innocence merely the absence

of experience?—i.e., can it be passive?
Or must it be willed? My friends
and I discuss this sticking-point one night. The moon
is pale, almost aqueous, and we're talking. Then
it's adamantly solid, like a throne-room gong
—we're talking. Then it's the ghost of a moon, already
almost lost in the approaching pearlescence of dawn.
It turns out we can travel assuredly through time
by simply sitting in our chairs or on the floor
and making lazy conversation. Just by having
a metabolism, we can voyage into the future.
Just by a pulse. By the immolation of calories.
The moon is a baby's nail-paring; the moon is the huge,
round resumé of the career of light; the moon is a curd of afterglow.
By the lines of a poem. By the chain of our breaths.
And Paula Volsky goes on to say:
                    But as she watched,
the face altered and aged, shifting through the phases
of adolescence, early and full maturity, middle age,
and thence to shallow old age.
                    An odyssey,
as surely as Ulysses' oceangoing is an odyssey:
but not by oars. By the blinks of an eye.

⟿

"In 1951, as Henrietta Lacks was dying of cancer in a Maryland hospital, one astute
physician there removed a pea-sized sample of her tumor to see if its cells would grow
in a test tube—something never achieved before—and these became the very first
human cells to thrive and multiply outside of the body. Now called HeLa cells, today
there are so many that they outweigh what would have been Henrietta Lacks's living
body 400 times, and have been used around the world in studies on polio, leuke-
mia, protein synthesis, the effects of nuclear radiation, genetic control mechanisms,
and more."

The sun has set, but the low and swollen
belly of the moon won't let its ruddy light completely
die out of the sky. So this will serve us as a symbol
meaning: we could end, right now, with the life
of Henrietta Lacks—and yet we can't, for Henrietta Lacks
has no immediate end. In life,
"her longest travel had been from her dirt-poor town
in rural Virginia, into Baltimore." In *after*-life,
"her cells were carried aboard the earliest space flights,
for experiments on zero-gees and cosmic ray bombardment."
Low and swollen moon—she's been there.

Moon of the gnashing wolf, moon of the overtumulting tidewaters,
moon of the itch of love, of the gnash of love, of the waters of love
—we've all been there.
Upstairs, my wife is sleeping; dreaming—what? How far
is the tether unraveled? If life is a stem,
by definition its flowering grows outside of the stem.
How short, how everyday, is the step
between two worlds?—the thickness of the skull? of the skin?
My wife's friend Jane's young son announced,
in case we didn't know it, "Men-have-penises.
Women-have-vagendas." That's a good one, yes?
And I've been pleased to have been issued passports
into some of those "vagendas"—to have traveled there.
And always, at that journey's end, I've been left breathless,
changed for a moment and lost in myself and breathless,
and beached on a foreign shore.

⌒

deer hoofprints, leading up to the river:
there, of course, they disappear

> *as we do, into the currents of sleep,*
> *of REM, of dream: eight hours*

and then continue on, as clear as ever
on the farther side

Tuvalu 〰

O where are the snows of yesteryear?
　　　　　　— Villon, *The Ballade of Lost Ladies*

Most U.S. high school seniors have a poor grasp of history . . .
57% of seniors could not perform at the basic level.
　　　　　　— *USA Today* coverage of a Department of Education report

Meteorologists will find interesting Vitruvius' description of wind
currents and, particularly, of the wind tower built at Athens by
Andronicus of Cyrrha.
　　　　　　— Marshall Clagett, *Greek Science in Antiquity*

1.

But my students won't—no, not if the wind
was the tiniest cry through needle-eye holes in the marble;
and not if it moaned through a hole as outsized as a human mouth
in agony; and not if the figure of bronze on top,
a great free-swiveling vane, was one of the gods
(and it *was:* Triton) . . . no, my students won't be interested,
my self-sequestered bubble-boys and -girls, so stuck
in the gluey streets of immediacy: last week, one sophomore
couldn't guess even the *century* of the American Civil War.
I'm the same with my wedding anniversary. Not one of us
is guiltless in this, "history" being synonymous
with "fuel"—and the present requiring constant motion.
Even subatomic condiments or rabbit-tracks or underwears—whatever
names the physics wizzes squeeze out of their brains these days—smash
into one another in enabling ways that newly recombine themselves,
although obliteration of their old selves is the price of this;
the music at the quarky heart of things is elegiac.
Now we can't walk on the moon without a valley
of mummies dissolving into fine Egyptian powder; can't
remarry without a fist of coal millennia old
unloosing itself as a one-hour rose of fire. When Pliny

the Younger reported his uncle's death at Pompeii, he added:
"These details are not important enough for history; you
will hear them without a true intention of saving them." He knew:
indifference buries us as surely as volcano ash.

2.

Tuvalu is starting to sink, that nation (population
about 10,000) housed for uncountable generations on nine atolls
600 miles north of Fiji—sinking, inches even as I write this.
Even now, the hungry licking of Pacific waves is coveting
the tava crops; and even now, "the places that were playgrounds
when we were children have disappeared"—Koloa Talake,
Tuvalu elder. "So eventually, in 50 years or so, the islands
will disappear. And the people there will also disappear,
along with their land." *Then* who will think to sing the praises
of the maidens and their dances of the coral-dragons' mating,
or record the words of the dying on "the final wings," those plaques
of scalloped shell? Who will remember the taste, or even
the *idea,* of tava? Every year, the World Memory Championship
is held in London (America's version is called the Memoriad);
the reigning heroes strut their mental stuff. Scott Hagwood
of Fayetteville, North Carolina, can exactly recall
"the order of a full deck of cards," and "a software engineer
from Alpharetta, Georgia" can reel off "a thousand-digit number
to the eighty-eighth place"*—but I have doubts
that we can pile sandbags of retention in a heap enough
to stop, or even slow, the slow erasure of the waters
as they seep across Tuvalu. And "Pompeii"—the *word itself* now

---

* 76959049004929774628416096696333215863309590544548374967370844100I-
5166758447512670720827.

is a flake of ash. "Charlemagne" . . . "Caravaggio" . . . "Sojourner Truth". . . .
The ocean giveth; it taketh away.
O, where are the shores of yesteryear?

3.

On Sixth in Austin, Texas, there's a combo bookstore (mystery, sci-fi)
which says (by way of this duality) how, for all of the lollapalooza kaboom
in inventing the future, there's an equal urge to reconstruct
and solve the past. It's what detective novels *do:* they fuss at what
took place; the least case—say, the rub-out of a cheeseball poolhall hustler
and his ho'—is still commemorative. Now tell me who
in 2002 will raise a small memorial to Fanny Burney's September 30th, 1811
mastectomy: with only "one wine cordial" for her anaesthesia, she endured
"the most torturing pain. I felt the knife rackling against the breast bone
—scraping it! cutting against the grain, attom after attom" until
"the air rushed into those delicate parts, and felt like a mass
of minute but sharp & forked poniards." This is the same one air
(well, duh: *there only is* one air, in its omniamoebic capacity) that
stroked the offered ankles of the lovers as they jutted
from a blanket on the sands the first night Coney Island opened;
is the air that bore the seeds of the London conflagration
Pepys reported: "So, with one's face in the wind you were almost burned
with a shower of Firedrops." Eventually the fire "was one entire
arch of above a mile long." Six hundred years ago. Now who
will weep, as Pepys did? For a while along the coast near Pompeii,
"the wind was full in my uncle's favor"—and Pliny the Elder
docked his ship. Already, the air was scalding char.
Elsewhere, dewy. Elsewhere, enraged. That wind
is our wind, as surely as it was Caesar's, Mahatma Gandhi's, Joan of Arc's.
It won't stop. Only we stop.

"Far": An Etymology ~~~

. . . in Georgia, if a ladybug's home is on far she sends for the farmen.

— Ogden Nash

"One who goes far ways": a way-"far"er; or sea-.
In 1950s sci-fi idiom: space-"far"er,
with its smug and zowie certainty that interstellar travel is
the farthest: so, the most heroic.
                              Oh really?
In the hospice Sara whispered something
soft and final into Neil's ear; from here it entered
into the featureless *terra mysterium* of his coma;
and *there,* for all she knew, it sailed itself to someplace out
of our physical universe altogether.
                              Who can tell?
We've mapped a pocky atlas of the moon's face,
of the ocean's deepest sweeps—yet if we try to be
subconsciousnauts, we lose ourselves to neural murk.
That handful in our skull might hold more distance
than the lights from the edge where our telescopes
shrug hopelessly and turn around for home.

And finally, what reserves
were drawn upon—and possibly depleted—for a small word of response
to start to form in Neil's mind? And what did time and space
require, for that word to make its pilgrimage
across his brain, across his tongue, and step out
into his room amid the flowers and nutrition tubules?
"Yes," he said. Just that, from out of a body of no.
For all she knew, his "yes" was a word in an alien vocabulary
that only coincidentally resembled a word of ours.

Our definitions, "goodness," "monstrousness,"
"euphoria," "sick pig-puke blues" . . . begin
with us, our own sweet center-of-all-of-the-cosmos selves, but

then approximate themselves how indiscriminately
to foreigners (read: "far"-eigners)
before they lose all meaningful applicability?
How many units-of-humaness away are we from being the saint
whose corpse "gave off the aroma of myrrh and honey
over four-and-forty days"? The saint whose life was such
that her body was finally borne, in death, to heaven
"on the breath of the angels of God's own Light and Mercy"?
—These are people who began as the same
meiotically rendered egg as you and me.
And of the "wicked men," the *chandalas* of India
that Fa Hsien writes about, "if such a man enters a town
he strikes a piece of wood, so to keep himself separate;
for on hearing this sound, the people know what it means, and they
avoid touching him or brushing against him" . . . he would be
in banishment as distant as the dark side of the moon.
What would it take for any "yes" to cross
that outer-space divide?
Although *I've* never heard them, Michael Cissell says
fish scream. He's seen his father slit
and start to gut one while
it's still alive . . . it screams then,
bringing it closer.

The Two Directions ～～○

Lucretius, too, attributes to the eyes the power
of actively extending—sending invisible beams
that grab the world and drag its nonstop images into our heads.
His busy, crisscrossed ancient Roman air
grows more familiar every day, from cell phones
to the SETI signals shooting our good wishes
and coordinates to otherworld receptor dishes we can only
guess at. One could come to think that all
we do is generate an outward radiation. But that would be
wrong, of course. It's as valid to posit our bodies in sleep,
my wife's and mine, as objects being worked upon
by time. I have a picture of an elderly Eskimo woman softening
leather in her mouth—for hours, saliva and tongue—until
its length of difficult grain can be shaped to the use she requires.

Ötzi ~~~

I sing of the fake claim to history
—the counterfeit tree
that says one's root is royal,
or holy, or undisputably native,
and therefore so is the current flowering
of that root. The hokey hominid,
the faux-ur sherd of Ark. I sing of the bogus crest of arms,
the forged certificate, the deep arroyo
salted with teeth from skeletons half a planet away,
with spurious jaws, with acid-tanned impostor-parts of skulls,
with knees that look like gray shells emptied of their oysters:
knees that figure in a court case now, to prove
or disprove ownerships, entitlements, exemptions.
I invoke the muse of genealogical hashwork, she
who duly presides over just such scenes as I've described;
I sing too of the poem, of the twenty-first-century poem,
that beckons the muse in this consciously ancient way
in hopes of calling down upon itself some semblance
of validity from a time when the words
were carved into stone, and intoned at the birthplace of prophets,
and worked into walls of pure gold.

~~~

My friends Shontelle and Denny are divorcing; all
of the "juicy sex" and "mutual support," become a house
of impossibly coexisting states: incendiary stares
and frozen air. I've written that *so* many times before,
about so many friends; in every instance, this is true:
each side attempts, with cunningly editorialized selections
from its memory, to rewire the past. Who promised what.
Whose so-called "pals" the (Blank)s were *really.*
How it was [through who] that the (blank) first entered their lives.
—And these establish lines of power

rich with time's authority: the present moment trembles.
This is why, in part, the sparring is so vicious.
It explains the night of open nail-gouges
down his face and a ripening vine of blueish bruises up her arm.
But of course: from all of their anger, precedent
is being invented. Out of *that,* the future is born
—*one* future; only one can survive. And this is why
the governments of Italy and Austria were locked in a proprietary battle
for the corpse that someone found in 1991, protruding from a glacier
at 10,000 feet in the snowily nebulous borderlands of the Tyrolean Alps
—looking like one outthrust fin of a beached sperm whale
of ice. And not just *any* corpse: "One of the greatest
archeological finds of the century . . . the world's oldest
preserved body of a prehistoric hunter, complete
with all of his clothes and equipment." That,
from Peter James's and Nick Thorpe's *Ancient Mysteries,*
which also archly terms the tug-of-warring "an undignified row"
between the two competing countries. Think of it as McHeritage:
whoever secures the earliest one,
forever owns the franchise.

⁓

And the straw that Shontelle added
to the camel's back of marriage was—a year before
they got their separate lawyers—her announcing how
"in a previous life" she'd been (she *always* had ambitious goals)
"Queen Nefertiti" ("NeferTEETEE"—Denny giving it
a nasally vulgar emphasis). Hey, *none* of us thought it was anything
other than nutty; still, at times a bad, deflating self-esteem
requires seeking out pneumatic kinds of lineage. If hers
seemed somewhat gaudier than most, and clearly artificial . . .
let her, we told him; *let her* retrofit her bloodline

into the dream of a dynasty, *so what?* But it was more than that,
of course; the cheap (and not-so-cheap) Egyptian kitsch
that slowly filled their rooms in tomb-of-Tutankhamen quantity
was only the latest symbol for him of a weight
they couldn't carry any longer. And the latest
of his own self-revelations? . . . he was gay,
he saw that now, and he'd been gay (if he'd just known it!)
from the beginning, he was gay down to his DNA, and here,
see, he could prove it with his new array of hosiery
and garterbelts . . . this didn't help
their rapidly faltering harmony *at all.* ("He'd made,"
as Shontelle said, "some swanky sets of satin teddy tops
and thongy bottoms that were better matches than we were.") Her
retrieval of her regal, diva ancestry was likely in response
to Denny's gender repositioning—though that's a causal timeline
he refutes in *his* account of their individual discoveries.
The two of them, endlessly jockeying for alpha-position in who
was transformed first. . . . I thought of him yesterday
as I browsed a book of Diane Arbus photos; one, of old-time
drag queens celebrating glitzed-up at a midnight spree:
not sleeker, wax-job, passable he-shes, but heavy men
who radiate a steak-and-baked-potato man-ness, shoved
—like feet too large in shoes too pinchy—into their glamorous
rhinestone-edged and fox-fur-trimmed decolletage. And what
of *this* one? . . . "Eliot revealed her identity in 1859,
after difficulties with a man named Liggins, who
was attempting to pass himself off as George Eliot": wow.
A man who thieves the identity of a man
that's really the pseudonym of a woman. *Unknowingly*
taking on the "other," the female self, that Denny
labored daily to fabricate with such intense devotion.

I sing of "Sheriff of Bullet Valley" (October 1948),
a comic-book story starring Donald Duck
as a shlemiel cowboy goodguy on the track of cattle rustlers
who mysteriously (it turns out, through the use of an "electro-ray")
imprint their pirate brand (a double X) across the diamond brand
belonging to a local honest rancher: this is done
with such a finely aimed congruency (just picture it), that
twenty madcap pages of the rootin'-tootin' kind
will gallop by, before this phony authenticity
is made known. And I likewise sing of the Kensington Stone,
that rune-replete (but ultimately failed) attempt to write
the Vikings onto America's pre-Columbus shores. And I sing
of the Cardiff Giant: epically proportioned ten-foot figure
out of gypsum, yes, but *not* (as its adherents insisted)
"an actual fossil of Biblical Man." Oh I sing,
and I sing, and the years slip past in singing,
and [include here a line
of Campbell McGrath's or Lucia Perillo's poems, as if
some keynote sensibility of mine, some signature fillip,
has been eaten by,
and digested into, a new and alien body].

Also that article in a recent *Harper's:*
no, there *wasn't* a sizeable population of Hebrew slaves
who toiled under the lash and jeers of the pyramid overseers of Egypt;
no, there *wasn't* a journey of forty years
through desert wastes . . . essentially, the priests of a people
fictioning together—out of ligatures of wish and of pure political need—
the history they required. Is this true?
Is *anything* "true"? King Arthur? Robin Hood?
An ancient nation of fierce female warriors? If we do believe
in a monotheistic God and His commandments: does it *matter*

if (in the lingo of security clearance) His background checks out?
And anyway, the further back
the background dendritically splits and links . . .
the more the ground is available
for anyone's appropriation: "Go back forty generations,
or about a thousand years, and each of us theoretically has
more than a trillion direct ancestors—a figure that far exceeds
the total number of human beings who ever lived. Confucius,
Nefertiti, and just about any other ancient historical figure
who was even moderately prolific must today be counted among
everyone's ancestors."—None of which shakes Shontelle's
certain faith in her "special relationship" (her words)
with Nefertiti. Pardon me: *Queen* Nefertiti. I saw her last
on a Mardi Gras float called "Nile Nights," surrounded
by a throng of loinclothed bodybuilder types
—"the Queen's attendants"—and waving overspillingly out at the crowd
from a low-cut asp-and-Nile-lotus-decorated bodice.
Strange, but . . . happy-strange. And how *much* she and Denny have
in common, now that they're apart! At least a taste in clothes.
I saw *him* last in a glitter-and-crinoline getup, partying
at one club's annual Boys Ball (for the record, it's the night
of the day they devote themselves to various charity projects).
He's so festive, which is so good to see, and the band
is so whompingly prideful and loud . . . for him I would bring
my ho-hum hetero self up to the mike, and I
would sing, and I would sing, and I would sing.

⌒

And even so, he'll argue with the lovers in his new life.
Shontelle, too. Me. You. It's like this: who
we think we are determines the whole of our narrative of the Earth
—and there will inevitably be conflicts.
A Viennese gay magazine disseminated the rumor

that radiocarbon tests performed on semen
discovered in Ötzi's anus—that was the name
the press had given to the prehistoric ice man,
after the valley uphill of his glacier—"identified him
as the world's oldest known passive homosexual."
We'll argue the Sphinx, and the huge impassive heads of Easter Island,
and we'll argue the very wax in our ears.
My wife and I attend the same neighborhood
potluck supper. This happens, that happens,
we love, we sleep, we wake, and when we speak again we see
there's no such thing as "a" neighborhood potluck supper.
At mine, I shone like a sun. At hers,
I exhibited fitful overcasts.
I call it Goldbarth's Law of Physics:
At the moment when the past becomes two futures,
it becomes two pasts.

A TRIP TO THE COUNTRY OF CRAZY, AND BACK

Heart Heart Heart Heart Heart Heart Heart

*"Oh, many a night my cousins and I spent out fishing and
sleeping under the stars—or with the bugs, as we used to say."*

⁓ a character in Sean Russell's *The Isle of Battle*

And that's the truth of it, the truth of the far perimeters
—the bugs; the stars—inside of which our little, loopy
human selves get lived; and lost; and led by rival vectors
of attraction way beyond our comprehension. Or not the whole truth,
no; the stars themselves are only showy speckling
on the ever-outward "surface" of an unknowable and invisible
veering-away; the insects? . . . symbolize the last of the apprehendables
before a faceless sub-ness starts, the micro without end.
No wonder we hold with such affection to the sky charts
of astronomy; to even *dilettantish* entomology,
its nets and pins. They make space seem to fit us:
I have a friend we found intoning one word scarily over and over until
she was lost, like a midge in a labyrinth: a mayfly in an oil drum,
out on the ocean, under the blown-open void.

⁓

"Self-inflicted injuries" as well. So she was locked up. And
she "came along," "progressed" in there, in finally understanding
how to master fear of what she called, as if it were her nemesis
and so had a campaign to wage, "The Shapelessness." For her, a certain
level of medication and therapy meditation "fixed her up."
For others, God: commandments and Heavenly hierarchies.
For others, anonymous serial sex: *anything* to act as a pattern,
anything to serve for rungs up all-too-empty air. And even
after she came home from the facility, she'd sometimes pick a sore
in her skin—her arm or her breast. "You see, the planet
is filled with all of these stunning potential jewels in its veins; but they need
to be dug out and given a form. That's how it is with beauty: it has

to be formed." The artful sore on her bosom, mauve and bright from damp
—in different light it might have passed for a brooch.

⟨～⟩

In early anatomical depictions—ancient Greek or ancient Arabic—
the world is still 2-D, and so we enter the cadaver as if
through opened doors in the thinnest chiffonier, of phyllo or rice paper
—here, our body's sweetbreads dangle like kindergarten cutouts on strings.
By the time of da Vinci, the tricky, miles-devouring perspective applied
to avenues of columns, or the sea, gets put to use on the sweep of our own
interior distinctions. The viewer now comes to see what the lover—spurned
or topsyturvily delighted—immemorially always knew: the heart holds
unlit mystery we float inside like spacemen lost to Earth. (So does the pancreas
and the intestines . . . although these organs don't play well in a poem.)
And when I said we found her "intoning one word over and over,"
that was (soon I'll tell you why) the word, her own nuts *om* of choice,
in which the sexual "tart" and the aesthetic "art" were also repeated
into a nonsense structure she was a gnat inside of, a fizzle of ash.

⟨～⟩

For some, the notion of "family." For some, to walk all seven of the Seven
Higher Righteous Paths of the Totem. Others, academic
rank. Creation science ["science"]. The fractal spread
of genealogical trees. If not for these, we'd have no guiding (check one)
)track)map)pole star)passion)overriding moral vision
)[add your own], and we'd be dropping through the nothing both
a major urban metroplex and a sesame seed are, under the rings
of their atoms. In a comic strip today, the phone starts shrilling;
the dog goes "Ruff Ruff Ruff"; the phone stops; and the dog thinks
"See? If you bark long enough, that thing shuts up." Yes, funny;
and pathetic. In one lovely 18th-century engraving,
the corpse's muscles from shoulder to butt are opened outward

like the petals of a rose: and we hold tightly to the ladder of ribs, for fear
of falling forever through this. For some, a sonnety fourteen lines.

⌒

Xoana, the shapeless primitive statues of gods.
　　⌒ *The New Larousse Encyclopedia of Mythology*

And if you ask my friends: the god inside themselves has come unshaped,
like clay after rain. The newspapers say it; the TV. We
have lost the definition of that part of us. That wonder
is xoana now; that power, that knowledge: xoana now.
Distress over this isn't shameful. "After the lecture, I was left
alone in the autopsy lab. I idly lifted the heart. I started
to peel it: the pericardium came off like the merest rubbery breath.
And then another layer. Another. At the center, there was a tiny entire
mummy, and I unwrapped it. And at the center of that: a jar
the size of a molecule, with a heart the size of a proton inside it,
and inside that was the autopsy lab of a midwest university
where a woman who had just been divorced was lifting a heart
to the light"—the place where everything beyond the stars
and everything below the insects . . . meet, becoming the other.

Scale-Model Sketch

For his birthday, they bought their ten-year-old
a pet boa constrictor. "Feeding time" became a matter
of knowingly kitschy ritual, with Marco Polo costumes
and a gold gong (*was* a trash-can lid). And then,
from a level about a thousand miles above this
sillihood, the snake would flow its glissando of ribs
around a corner, survey its domain and—somehow
without an indication of speed or even movement—
gulp the living mouse down whole. *That's* the way
the topless dancer devoured my bachelor friend J.W.
(however—to be fair—he'd placed himself there
very willingly). The similar, seemingly
boneless, sway of the body. The laden line
of contact, eye to eye. The trance. The ceded power.
Something earlier than language, something
chromosomal. And then he was gone, entirely
and instantly, although, from then on,
it played itself out in a slo-mo series
of ten-dollar tips, then fives, and ones, until
she wore a holster of money on either hip,
and by the furry malt-light of last call, they
were playfully bonded for quarters: I saw her
finally sit in his lap with a penny centered
ecstatically on her outstretched tongue—it looked then
like the full moon I saw
float in the throat of water in a clay jar,
on my back stair once, in a Mexican village
so small that I always thought a rain
of more than an hour would wash it into the jungle
totally, one telephone, a butchering knife, and five flutes
riding a handful of silt. And why
I was there?—the skin I'd been born into
wasn't enough, I guess; its far-outfurling mesh

of connections wasn't enough. I wanted more
inside me, more digestion stones, the way the owl has,
and more for them to go to pulverizing
work on. I remember that I walked out
to the back stair, past the jar, to the yard, and
listened for the first time to a night of the world
unmasked of anything urban, even anything vaguely
neolithic. Only the zipper-like, rivery rush of a few
Goliath centipedes in under-underbrush.
A shriek—with wings. The liquid whickering of something
in the grip of something else; and then
the slobber of the something else. The whole dark
is alive with jewels of blood, as if
(in species-centric likening): the blueprint,
or correlative, or prototype, or scale-model sketch,
of our own human hungers.

A Knife through the Head (Your Distresses and Mine)

When Nona phoned, her stomach was already little more
than a gourd of blood, from the pills; and so I talked
across 500 shaky miles, until she finger-gagged
the puke up. I don't know the technical definition
of "clinical depression," but I believe her: every single
stinking object in the world was saying *useless* to her,
every ivory vase had that much hurtful
personality, the condiment dish, her attaché case,
her purse comb with its mouseballs of hair in the teeth. . . .
I'll never understand the reason it's "pathetic," this natural
fallacy the brain produces as readily as any other perception
(see line three: the miles are "shaky"); and surely it works
in joy as well as in despair: to the googoo couple in love,
the hardware store is filled with googoo hardware. Or

the rather ramlike bas-relief faces of Babylonian gods
are really the faces of Babylonian believers: how could it be
otherwise? The almond-eyed Egyptian gods, the same.
The props-room beard of the avuncular God of Bible Camp.
The shorty-pants-and-goggles Mouse Himself:
when Mickey takes to the skies in *The Mail Pilot* (1933),
his gesso-white geishalike face and its puttyesque
black brow enact an overboiled doubletake version of your
distresses and mine, and when he mashes
the aeronautical brakes in panic or other cartoon concern, his
two-seater mail plane bucks like a doubled-up hot dog.
Yes—what art is all about. The background is gray,
is weightily gray, so the man by the bay is melancholic,
etc. A rainbow: the shepherdess is happy. In Art Therapy

at the Clinic today, we have a man with a tripe-knife through his head
as done by a man who has a tripe-knife through the head
inside his head. We have a woman with a lavender hoodoo light
exploding like a neon geyser from out of the toothy smile
that replaces her crotch. Another woman is calling such power
down from Heaven, it's licking all over her naked goddess body
like adders' tongues, if adders could be plugged in a row
of electrical sockets and made to give off grinder's-wheel sparks.
One man, in a stellarscape of novas and cankered planets,
displays his asshole as if it's a ring on a white silk pillow:
eyes spew out. One woman is nothing but a red penny-sized dot.
And these are all Nona. *Everything* is Nona. She enters
the Clinic's front door and it's only one more
room in the world of a thousand selves of the one self.

The Feelers

His plays scourge our society. A two hour monologue literally flattened me
by the end, and in fact did *bring on a fever, so that I had to lie down,*
while others showed him out of my apartment.

— from a confidential letter of recommendation

1.

A brick is floating around the room
as slowly and as proudly
as a show horse in the rodeo ring,
and then————————————
it crashes into the window *Jesus* everybody
ducking flying shards. They look at the mess
with a quiet awe (it's not their only creepy misadventure
with a levitating object)—the mother, the father,
the boy and the girl, and this one time
two wild-eyed, incredulous,
shit-frightened dinner guests. They absolutely
slather the brick with their stares
and unasked questions: yes, but the brick
in its lei of powdery glass isn't giving
up any secrets.

In another place: that flat stone
(where the corn gets ground) is hurtling through
the grass-woven front of the hut.
Another: the smashing of seven (seeming very heavy, ceremonial)
goblets—one at a time: deliberately—from an attic
where no goblets are stored; this happens
for three consecutive nights.
Another: "Every time we left the house
we were pelted by gravel. Toren suffered
open cuts on one occasion; and a weathervane

got knocked to the ground by the force of it. But
no one could ever see where the gravel originated,
it just *appeared.* And no one could see,
not even in the clearest of day,
who threw it."

⁓

The people who study these phenomena
[*polter*, "knocker," "rattler"] have determined
that almost always a child is present in the afflicted household,
normally an adolescent (sometimes it's a child on the cusp
of adolescence) and it's typically a girl,
the one most "sensitive," the peeled nerve.
And this isn't a house where an axe is surreptitiously
hidden under a bed, or an inner
bulimial fire eats a person from her gutside out
. . . nobody here is weird that way, nobody
here is anything other than neighborly and filial.
Except sometimes they come home to discover
the living room covered in fecal smears.

⁓

And the father was fat with a sexual hunger.
The mother was fat with an old, old hurt.
The brother was fat with the need to be cruel
to anything handy—a bird, a limping newspaper boy.
And the girl . . . the daughter, sister . . . she
was the wick. The fatness entered her,
it mixed with her own hormone-fat,
and she burned . . . she burned, for all of them.
What units do we measure this by?
A gust of gravel. A grinding-stone.
Seven exploding goblets.

2.

In one novel of the "alternate Earth" variety,
every business, government office, and private
residence of the wealthy has its "feeler": a specialist
designated the weeper, the giddy gibberer,
brooder, fumer, dreamer, hoarder of perceived slights
in his social sphere, so that all of its other inhabitants
can stay free of what's thought to be,
in that world, a debility. "He's someone,"
as we used to say in an English Department I worked at
(this, in reference to a secretary named Dan) "who could think
of the impact craters cankering the moon,
and feel guilt." Whatever hurt might play its way
through our community and then depart . . .
would still remain for days in his saliva;
in the lush, irrupted lining of his mouth;
in a rash that lingered on his hands
—as if milking an encore.

When a month of what Tina and Andi considered standard
wicked banter found him heaving one morning
in sobs on the neck of a student who'd simply come in
for a change-of-grade form . . . Dan was fired
immediately, no one-week-notice or "medical leave."
And *now* who'd be the easy butt of Phelps's sawtooth wit?
(Who's Phelps?—the brother from section 1, the childhood
torturer of kittens: but grown up to be a bitter associate prof.)
Now who would serve as his own special low-wage whipping boy?
Not Dan. Nor did we remember him much: by April
he was only a half-used tube of shingles ointment
someone found behind the xerox toner.
                                        There,

you see the difference? On that other Earth
he'd have his private office, and be honored
for the difficult specifics of his service.
Yes, and maybe in that other world, because of this
the rest of us could go about our business with a pride
in the depth and the quality of those feelings
which he admitted for us.

⌒

Often in tribal societies that's all
the shaman, the "healer" of the culture, really does: he *feels*
richly (or say "neurotically" if you want to),
anther, barometer, fuse. Sometimes,
along with a tea from the leaves of the shield-bark tree
and a little chanting, nothing else is needed
for the general ongoing health of a people.
Maybe we *should* have corporate feelers;
federal; local; domestic. It would only
give official recognition to the fact
that in a group—or in a duo, even;
in a marriage, even—*someone's* stomach
will record a more emphatic graph of any day's events,
in an open, ulcerous line on the wall there.
In a flare of hives. The red web in the eyes.
Someone's asleep—and someone else is up
at the window, watching the few cars left
at 3 a.m. as they rush to somewhere, carrying
bodies of moonlight on their fenders.

3.

And someone is Gemma Galgani,
whose "stigmata began as red marks; then
a fissure would open slowly beneath the skin,

until finally the skin tore open, revealing
the cavity filled with congealed and flowing blood.
This happened every Friday, and the hole
would be healed by Sunday." There are affidavits,
"independent testimony," the works. Some
show their flesh raised in the size and shape of the nails
hammered through Him; some display a ridge
like a ring on the appropriate finger: "a bride of Christ."
In the 800 years since the death of St. Francis,
"some 500 cases are documented, of individuals
clearly and repeatedly exhibiting the definitive signs."
Often, the world is too much for them: Anjelica Azzari
was pained by ordinary daylight and by ordinary sounds,
and "her face was never washed clean of the blood
she wept: she could not bear the touch of a cloth and water."

⁓

But wounds of the Crucifixion are only one choice
on the psychosoma menu. What if every small
embarrassment created a blush that lingered
for days in the shape of its cause?
If every flush across the chest of orgasmic completion
were worn there like a crimson-stippled scarf?
That isn't likely, no; but crank it up
a notch on the human drama machine, and then
indeed we do have the eleven-year-old "peasant girl"
Eléonore Zugun, of Roumania, who in 1923
"began suffering bite-like marks spontaneously appearing
over her face and neck, from no external agency
discernible even during her observation in London
under controlled conditions." Or the "unnamed man"
in London in the 1950s who, when he'd relive
"a traumatic episode from his past, when he had been

tied with ropes," would soon show, "under the gaze
of his doctors, the unmistakable indentations
of tightly bound rope on his arms."

⌒

Now this is the part where you
enter the poem. You heard me:

you. Are you the one asleep?
Or are you the one at the window?

—watching the traffic, counting the stars,
repeating the sores and injustices,

and then staring down at the pulse-point
where your blood is a whisper inside of your wrist:

stigmata waiting to happen.

4.

> Some years ago, Nigel Kneale wrote a TV play called The Stone Tape *in which*
> *far-distant events of an extreme nature literally imprinted themselves into stones*
> *—rather like records on modern tape.*
>
> ⌒ from the letters column of *The Fortean Times*

I share that with you because of the afternoon
the office door stormed open, there was a nightmare
scuffle of scream and gunfire, and then:
a number of flesh wounds spurting gore.
The expert for the defense said Dan
was "a victim of hyper-aesthesia, and other forms
of over-receptivity"—so, when he was fired,
"it darkened his mind." (Did *anyone* believe this

should exonerate attempted murder?) And while two stalwart
graduate students wrestled him pinned to the floor
and tore the weapon from his rashy hands
—two women, each, I swear, weighing under
a hundred pounds—our big-talk, cock-walk bully Phelps
was cowering under a back-room desk (and also,
according to next day's rumor, whimpering
and soiling his pants). So:
which man was the "most sensitive"?

I can't make a slippery judgment like that.
Ask centuries of water,
of wind, of uric acid, ask Nigel Kneale:
even stone is impressionable.

THE EVERYDAY DYNAMICS OF FLIGHT

27,000 Miles

These two asleep . . . so indrawn and compact,
like lavish origami animals returned

to slips of paper once again; and then
the paper once again become a string

of pith, a secret that the plant hums to itself. . . .
You see?—so often we envy the grandiose, the way

those small toy things of Leonardo's want to be
the great, air-conquering and miles-eating

living wings
they're modeled on. And bird flight *is*

amazing: simultaneously strength,
escape, caprice: the Arctic tern completes

its trip of nearly *27,000* miles every year;
a swan will frighten bears away

by angry aerial display of flapping wingspan.
But it isn't all flight; they also

fold; and at night on the water or in the eaves
they package their bodies

into their bodies, smaller, and deeply
smaller yet: migrating a similar distance

in the opposite direction.

Five Pounds 〜

This non-aerosol prayer dates from the forties.
〜 *The Inside Collector*

1.

But aren't *all* prayers aerosol?—they leave
in a breath, and rise *through* air, *as* air,
until they finally reach an Ear of Ears, a Hearing, which
is even more invisible and ubiquitous than oxygen.
—A six-year-old's sweet notion. But they took me,
when I turned thirteen, to a bare-plank
storefront synagogue for the annual Day of Atonement.
Here, the men who had already fasted
near to twenty hours, standing all this time,
incanting tearfully . . . their exhalations had the sour weight
of bile acting as a brake upon ascension.
This was a lesson in the true, long, heavy dumbbell heft
of penitence—in Godward imploration as the Brie-smell of a foot
too long in its shoe. One man was rolled in
on a wheelchair, then lifted from it, and set on the floor
on his waist—his way of standing. There he was,
a squatty mound of a creature, fastened to the ground
without a minimal inch of vertical direction anywhere on him
. . . and singing; wringing out those grief-lined songs
as loudly as anyone—louder,
from the handicap
of extra air to rise through.

2.

"Airy," "breathy"—these are the words
we use to talk about the mind
imploring "God" (or "gods" or "Fate" . . . whatever)
in its purest transcendental state.
But given who we are, we also need

to preserve, and disseminate, and regularize
. . . and so the prayer must be given a physical body.
On a stone. On fired clay. On sheets of the beaten
marsh plant of the Nile. Of course when we think
of monasterial effort—all of those rows
of thickly ebony letters with a kind of undeniable,
writhing, tuber-like presence; and then the occasional
peacock-glory spray of carnelian and gilding—it's
on parchment and vellum: "the skins of almost all
the well-known domestic animals, and even of fishes,
have been used"—as they were, in that same time,
for the earliest condoms. Interesting:
"prayer," "sex"—the same availability employed
for both transmission and prevention.
(Plus, that famous wedding of prayer and sex,
"Oh God. Oh God. Oh God.")

3.

A man is pumping gassy plumes of "Bug-Kill"
in the gnatty room, at a host of midge-like
swoopers and soarers that make the light
kaleidoscopically lovely—though this man
is in "a snit," "a very devil of a temper," and dances
frantically about as if he's holding in a pantsfull. . . .
I have to tell you that the typo in the text
I've used for my epigraph is a dropped "s": "sprayer"
—a cumbersome, very industrial-looking, all-metal thing
(like what would maybe be a perfume shpritzer
on The Planet of Giant Robots). It's the kind of device
we think of as the prop in an especially slapstick scene
from a 1940s "screwball comedy": you know, the type
where he loves her, and she loves him, with all
of the loftier sentiments the human breast can bear

—sublimity, spiritual longing, self-sacrifice—but hurdles,
contretemps, and an irascible tycoon parent
have been placed in their way, requiring that the progress of this young love
be conducted as a series of ridiculous disguises,
furtive smooches, merry-go-roundish chases, yapping dogs,
and pies-in-the-face. So here's our guy
with such exquisite aspirations yearning for expression,
and he's hopping around with this five-pound sprayer
brandished like a blunderbuss. A man
and his burden, tied to the earth.
And that cloud, with its skin of a thousand wings.

The Sign*　～

Another poem that starts with geese across the sky
at the end of a day—the second when
its brightness is finally stubbed out on the horizon line.
Now there's more sun on the bellies of these geese
than anywhere else in the world altogether. Incandescent.
Freshly smelted ingots—flying.
Then they dim. They're gone. It's the way
of the *erev* to only last for a moment.

　～

Did they know, that Saturday night, in the fire
of quickened nerve-end pleasure, in their roll-around hour of sweet,
sweet sex adventure . . . did they foresee
what was started? Well,
no: it took a few months. And thirteen years
from then, in all of the soulfulness and gaiety
that attached to their only child's *bat mitzvah*
(she was at the lectern, and delivering
a toast to her guests: officially now an adult
of the tribe), could they look back and understand
that flash of reddish orange neon on their dampened bodies
(*Sunset Time Motel:* like an external pulse)
with every shivering breath
was a sign of the *erev?*

　～

John asked me: Would I be writing about it?
I didn't know. It seemed right to, of course.
It also seemed an inexhaustible jinx—to fix this thing

---

* Traditionally, Jewish holidays begin at sundown of "the day before": this is *erev* Passover,
erev Yom Kippur, etc.

in written language, offered publicly; and since
it *had* turned out, here, on the other side
of a week of nightmare worrying, to be benign . . .
wouldn't I be positioning myself to one day seek out
and reread that diagnosis in the bitterly ironic light
of later, unluckier news? A week before, John underwent
his own "procedure" and, a stranger as he was
to the medical rituals, stepped out innocently from the prep room
in a gown he'd tied on backwards. "I think
from now on, it's a series of increasing humiliations
for us"—John's my age, fifty-five. Okay,
so let their bloody knife-work on my frightened and flickering
chickadee-of-a-prostate
usher in that age.

⁓

The instant when the sun entirely disappeared
except for them . . . something like those memorizers
in Bradbury's *Fahrenheit 451.*
Working to keep the dazzle alive, the way that "phantom limb" does.
And I heard them, first—the honking.
Then the arrow-tip they shape up there, in flight.
I suppose to a literalist, they're geese.
But to a student of the seasons, they're an announcement.

⁓

I was telling Mark the plumber about my little
invasive drama. He was on his back,
the better to reach the S-pipe under the kitchen sink,
and I watched his body involuntarily shrivel up
into a parody of the fetal position.
He's fifty-three. He doesn't want to go there.

But he's going there. My story is a door
he'll have to walk through.

⌒

My mother was at the *bat mitzvah.* Of course:
these are friends of ours. "Such a WONDERFUL time."
She even danced in her rose-petal gown
with a slightly tipsy military retiree
who dipped her over his arm as if she might be
seventeen again, not seventy, and every year
a feather, a giggle, a bubble of champagne.
Her coughing started that night. It was there
when she kissed the *bat mitzvah* girl on the cheek,
and when she finished the last
of her cigarettes and gave a sweetly sloppy good-bye to the parents,
and a check. In a week, the oncologists were starting her
on a regimen of the chemical immolation
that they thought (but were wrong) would halt her own
interior burning. "Now I'm going"—she had always been good
at saying big things simply. "Going": yes,
migrating as far as we can, although
she didn't move along the hospital bed by a single lateral inch.
And now I wish we had a photograph
of her rose-petal night at the punch bowl,
lifting the hem of her dress so she could all the more riskily sleek
across the floor to the lame sax of that mediocre band.
I wish we had a photograph: we don't. We didn't know
this was the difficult, slag-light, flame and ash-pit
beauty of the *erev.*

Vacation: Carolina Coast

Maybe it's because we're all born into this world
on a wing of blood, that we can't stop from seeing our lives
in sunrise on the water.
                              Of course enough of us leave
in violence, that sun*set* is also powerful
metaphorically. Enough of us sink out of this world
still burning, still believing
that the night is long, but passes.

One day a distracted gull got into the beach house,
through the front door, as if it were a rightful tenant.
That was its attitude, in fact, for the whole
two-hour comic opera chase: that somehow *I*
was the one who simply was renting this space
for a little while.

date: the late 1770s
Unable to secure financial backing
for his telescope, and undeterred, the avid
William Herschel made the necessary molds himself
from horse shit. With that finished apparatus,
he could see "the farthest stars,
the highest, and most angelically rarefied
aerial show." As with this gull:
                              this garbage feeder,
picker of offal,
eater of gutter dung, that rises
into the clear empyrean.

J. phoned today. Among the news:
that D. and M. are separating.
"Look, these things happen. It's difficult,"
she said, "for poet-and-poet marriages."
Yes, I suppose. Although you might think,
to look out my window, that water and water
are easily—are perfectly—water.
What better formula *is* there?
You might think . . . well, anything you or I
or A. or Q. or T. or K. might think
in our glib metaphors isn't the point
now anyway. And sometimes out my window, they say,
there are storms that can drive a whole house apart.

I must have been standing in front of a scrap
it desired, because the gull looped down
in front of me, eye level—we were truly
nose to beak—and, by some avian magic,
hovered there immovably without needing
to scull the air at all. One of us had
to yield the way and, after some rapid thinking,
it was me. I wasn't out there to make
a living; the gull had greater claim.

And Herschel saw "a magnitude of stars,
in such array beyond our counting, I was lost there
like a child in a strange land." What we do is make of them
a throne, a swan, a cup to dip with; even a dragon
is something relatively familiar.
                                    On the intercoastal
waterway, the surface can be calm enough to see

the sky—the way a lover bends to the face
of a lover, and sees a version
of his own face there. That must be a thing we do
for each other: make ourselves seem somewhat
comprehensible.
                "The anus, the urethra, and the vagina
were once called 'the other face': an appropriate name
for mock eyes, noses, and mouths"
(James Elkins). —Constellating
the terrifying and wondrous into something we know.

        ⌐⁓

Ooo yumyum, food. Ooo, zero-in, food.
You have to live around them a while
to truly understand the etymology:
gull: gullet.

        ⌐⁓

At one point, shore becomes a stony tendril
extending into the ocean. Follow this, eventually
you're standing on the dot below a question mark
—just you, a rock beneath you,
and an endlessness of blue that goes down to Atlantis
and up to the coalsack black of outer space.
It ends here; there's no further step to take.
Except . . . it sometimes seems there *is*. I don't mean
drowning; or astral projection; or anything that
dramatically metamorphic. But: isn't there an inch
beyond, that's still you . . . but a fog of you,
a foam of you . . . a you that isn't beat every day
by the whisk of waking up human. . . .

        ⌐⁓

Of hundreds of luscious and nearly naked
nineteen-year-old tanners on this beach, the one
whose poses take my wildly roving fancy
deepest into her is a woman with an arrogantly careless
squat, her ass become the reckless cleft
a fuschia thong's slim, spandex grip accentuates . . .
ooo, yumyum: girl; ooo, zero-in: girl.
                                        Is *this*
what happened to D. and M.?—this common greed
monogamy won't tolerate. Or could it be more
complicated?
                —one of them *did* get within reach
of stepping into a fog-self, into a foam-self,
and (so often the case) was frightened by it,
or bored by it, was faced with a self
too alien, and so there was no antidote
but running back to the messiest part
of being human again.

        ⌒

Now Spring has returned, enticing boats
to dance upon the waves once more . . .
                        —Antipater of Sidon,
in *The Greek Anthology* [X : 2].
Here, they're lined up in the marina:
The Atomic Balm; Tight Tooshie; Tax Break;
Bix Dix; Sea Slummer; Elvis Lives.
Spring has returned, and the boats are enticed,
and a tang of eternity spices the harbor.
Maybe Elvis *does* live. This is the same and patient
algae that coated the pilings when the *Argo* gave weigh.

        ⌒

And was it my father who called to me,
into my sleep? No, it was a boat's horn
in the drizzling distance; my father is even farther
than that, farther, farther, farther than that.
And was it myself, from when I was a child,
yelling through my dreams? No, it was only another
squawking gull on the jetty, one of hundreds.
And then it wasn't the ancestors? it wasn't the muses,
wasn't the Otherworldly Powers advising me
through wind, and the boards, and the rigging? It was
wind, and the boards, and the rigging.
And yet. And yet, on a day that follows a night
of such wide-open supposition, a man can walk the pier
and see his thousandth cliché gull of the season,
only a speck in his peripheral vision, and somehow
nonetheless be zapped with the thought
—it might be a wind, or a distant horn—
that something important is always folding
into itself, is dough into dough, eggwhite into eggwhite,
cloud into air, storm into silence,
life into cloud, death into rain, egg into a rising dream of waking.

Out, one brisk azure afternoon
with Mark on his boat the *Misty C.*
The churn of water behind us
breaking, and healing; breaking, and healing;
splitting, and wedding, and breaking, and healing.

THROUGH HISTORY ON PENNIES A DAY: 1

Branches

A vagina in the center of the pomegranate
Dante Gabriel Rossetti paints in the hand of Jane Morris.
And the pomegranate that holds the name of God
in a cursive swirl of its tissues and seeds.
Those two would be enough to tell us that the world
is not monocular. The woman saying look at this,
meaning the thing. The man saying look at this,
meaning its shadow. And from that,
if conjectural physics is right, the universe branches
into two. Exalting, on the level of cosmology.
On the level of communication across a bed,
it's a dauntingly wearying day. Remember
the linen strip inscribed with a fragment of ancient
Roman poetry? They found it in a mummy,
in a scrim of crackled oil under the chest.
A treasure—rescued from oblivion! To someone, once,
it was rubbish to wad inside an empty heart-case.

Patoot and Poopik

"Weal" is a good word, and especially wedded tight
to its alliterative phrase-mate, "woe," like
"thick and thin," "do or die," etc. We don't use it
anymore, I don't know why. It might be something like the physics
that we know applies to people: so we can't gain "wonky,"
"dot-com," "homeboy," "gravitron," without the death
of "orrery" and "wastrel" and "greaves" and "sillibub."
And call this an economy of language; call it verbal
evolution; whatever, *the future* is going to call it
—and here we have to leave a blank. Nobody knew my sister's
child would be "Ian" until our father died in her eighth month
and she chose to continue the I of "Irving" that way. Now when

I think of him—that open, industrious, decent man
in his flop-around thrift-shop skivvies—an entire antiquarian world
of lost jaw-music surfaces; it's like the poker banter of Atlantis
rising back again into the discourse of the world. "She's got
a face like a horse's patoot." "That guy?—a real nogoodnik,
a fourflusher. Give him the bum's rush." When he'd lecture me
on what it meant to be a man, while I was someone clearly past
a "pisher" and a "pipsqueak" and yet not the fully capable
thoughtful "mensch" he hoped I'd be . . . his good intentions
slid from me "like water off a duck's—" (as he'd
complete it:) "keester," "poopik." And although linguistic
history allows for the nostalgic resurrection of some words

(which I call "reinventing the weal"—ha!), I simply don't believe
his "cockamamie" or his "tootsweet" or his specialty,
"bassackwards," is about to shuffle amazedly out of the graveyard,
reelectrified with a new conversational currency. If anything,
some doddering vocabulary *needs* to disappear, we have

so many words by now. Every one of the six or seven souls
that the Inuit say exist "like tiny people scattered
throughout the body" . . . has a name. The cockroach breathes
through rows of "spiracles." And "the energy a proton would acquire
while being accelerated across a voltage drop
of a billion volts" . . . ?—this is a "GeV." So many.
More than a googol, I bet. And yet, there's not a word for what

I felt when I entered the hospital room and saw his livid,
cathetered cock; for what vise squeezed my heart
when he opened the bedroom door and caught me masturbating;
for the choking when my penny-ante grade-school prize
elicited a pride in him a rajah's ruby couldn't buy.
In front of these, our tongues recede and fail.
—As after his usual lecture, he would usually sigh
(and here they all, at once, crash through me in a helpless tumult,
paternoster, heebie-jeebies, animalcule, scrip, legerdemain,
malarkey, janissary, antimacassar, poosk, quidnunc)
and observe in a voice so woeful, it kneeled: "Albie,
you don't understand a single word I'm saying."

Into That Story

1.

It's dawn. The ancient Greek warriors strap on
their armored shielding. Of course to them,
there, then, in the itch and the juice
of their lives, they aren't "ancient"—aren't even "Greek,"
but loyal members of a city-state. The members of a different one
await them, on the far side of a pearly, swirling fog
they have in common. Now our warriors are marching
grimly into that opacity: it takes the man ahead,
and then the man behind, as surely as an enemy ambush would.
Dissolved—like aspirin mixed in milk.
And so—although surprise would be a clever tactic—
now they're singing: someone else might say they're echolocating,
relative to the other men of the corps. But I would say
that what they're doing is simply reminding themselves
they're them, here, now—they *aren't* fog, not yet,
one has a stone in his sandal; one, the taste
of a wife still in his beard. They're doing what
everyone does, who isn't fog, not yet. I suppose
this writing is my singing.

2.

"Throw him into a room on the funny farm,"
Uncle Les said of the "neighbor boy" as they called him,
Marv, "and he'd blend right in.
Like spit on cum." And then a sharp awareness
of my presence—I was six—and everybody stared up into ceilingspace,
fidgeted, and grew mum. Marv
must have been at least sixteen,
but didn't shave yet, talked to himself, was never seen
without a baseball glove, and talked to the glove,
and handled the glove with weird familiarity.

"Not funny ha-ha," my mother said, to both
deflect attention from her brother's salty mouth, *and*
as a cautionary lecturette.
"Funny don't-*ever*-go-near-that-guy."
but nothing, even back that far, rerouted me
away from words that had the jazz.
Like spit on cum.
Language like that you don't forget.

3.

Except we do forget.
It's fifty years since then.
A car drives into the fog and disappears
like—something.
Like something on something.
Snow in sleet . . . aspirin . . . milk. . . .
"Like dew in rain"? Those warriors,
from section 1 . . . for centuries, their helmets
were assumed to be the drinking-cups of gods.
Why not? The warriors themselves by then
were—something. Snow in fog.
A person—da-da-da-da,
something something. *In a gene pool,* yes.
A person in a gene pool.
In the haze. In the blur of the smudge-pots.
In the evaporating touch of the sun.
When a deer's strung up, and first slit,
and the guts tumble out, it almost seems
that the body is *eager*
to lose its definition.

4.

And even at six, I knew the neighbors'
sixteen-year-old daughter radiated a dangerous aura,
hormonal and non-stop. ("Dangerous" here
is code for "yank-by-the-nose compelling.")
I would sneak peeks at her oil-slathered tanning
in their backyard—every inch down, from the browning cups
between her neck and shoulders, to the lovely
seahorse-bodied curl of her toes—and then,
on date nights, I would marvel at the way that tan
so knowingly counterset a diamond pendant. Since
she died that year, she's *still* sixteen,
though fifty years have passed. Although another way
of saying it: she's fifty years towards being,
after some interim stages, diamond herself.
We're all tomorrow's fossil fuel, that's certain.
Once we say it that way, at least we can predicate
where the body goes. As for the rest . . . where does the name
of a daughter, husband, grandson, go to
when it dwindles on out of the collandered mind
of a panicked, nursing-home Alzheimer's patient?
Snow—was that it? Fog—was that it?
Dinosaur: gas tank: emissions—is that it?

5.

In *someone's* version of four missing days, the aliens
snorfled her up to their hovering mother ship
in a fingersnap; undid the outermost layer of her skin
with the ease of rubbing adhesive off of a price sticker;
rearranged a few organs, temporarily; invasively probed, and studied her
most intimate throbs and flows; replaced the skin,
which fit as perfectly as ever; and then returned her

(naked) into the midst of a picnic at a nudist colony
where, one assumes, she blended in—from the point of view
of an extragalactic alien—indistinguishably
from the rest of the short-lived human globs:
like spit on cum. With this same guiding theory,
errant spouses, and runaway teens, and spies
with enemy counterespionage implacably on their tail
simply lose themselves in bustling crowds of similar selves;
snow, aspirin, mist. The rich availability
of metaphors for this! The moth,
invisible against a ground of jungle moss and guano.
The corpse, thrown overboard into the ocean, *is*
—at first in molecular stages and then entirely—the ocean.
Tomorrow, my wife knows, she'll be giving herself
to the long demands of a dark day . . . and already
as she tries to sleep (with only intermittent success),
she begins to adjust, and she softens
into the melanin of the evening.

6.

But it wasn't a deer
I was talking about in section 3;
that scene served as a tolerable replacement
for the more difficult one of a human body
hung up by the wrists and tied at the ankles
and opened the same way, with a saw-edge blade
as smoothly through the muscles
as if they were soap or cheese, and the guts
spilling out as if they'd been impatiently waiting for this
all along. Our soldier from section 1—the slightly
more likeable fellow; the one with the wife—
has witnessed this scene: not, obviously, as its victim,
and not as its perpetrator, but close enough

for the reek of that gaping cadaver to overpower even
the stink of his own fear. He's seen much more than that,
and worse than that—a kind of devil's lesson book
in how the body melts into the world—
and now, so many adventures later,
we find him back at home, at the side of his wife
as she's asleep, her middle (month eight) looking ready
to burst at any moment. What
conflicting glories and depredations coexist in his head
as he lets his hands crabwalk across
the radiant heat of that belly?

7.

A light wave. What? A kiss, a "French kiss," sloppy
and deep. Where? What? The war—or "a" war: how
to count them, there are so many? The bird. What
bird? You know, I saw it in the—mist, in the snow,
in the rain on the lake. So many things, and so much time,
and when we go back, has *anything* been impervious
to subatomic flux? And yet I think I *do* remember
the knock on the door with a steadfast clarity.
I was six, maybe seven. My mother answered, and talked
to the men on the front porch, then she called my father.
Something about the neighbor girl—the neighbor girl
and Marv. There was a quiet anger to some of these men,
and a few of them looked ashamed. One held
a baseball bat. My mother looked frightened,
she didn't seem to realize I was in the room. Frightened
and. . . . resigned, I suppose. Anyway, that's how
I see it now. And when my father conferred with the group,
he joined them, there on the porch: he hugged my mother,
then turned his back, and walked off
with those oddly quiet men, to do what had to be done,

no matter how disproportionate
to the life of our house as we lived it daily.
I see him still: walking into the night,
until he and the night are indivisible.
Finally, he's an electron of night.
Whatever story is waiting out there . . .
already, he's dissolved into that story.

Geese Jazz ～

And time, that river, erodes away
the banks of the present moment, it carries us
all in its current. God,
did *I* write that? Did I *write* that?
The boy-who-thought-he-was-a-man
in the natty Nehru jacket and love beads (1968),
with Phyllis on his mind (and very elsewhere too)
and poesy's strains like a great storm in his heart
. . . did he write *that?* Needs change.
"Vibes" change. The zeitgeist trembles,
falls a thousand miles, and reinvents itself
on titanium wings. "Great storm in his heart"?
Oh jeez. My Nehru sartorialness was formerly
. . . what? In 1828, a flurry of election campaigning
found Martin Van Buren attired in "a beige and elegant
swallow-tailed coat with matching velvet collar,
pearl-gray waistcoat, orange cravat (with lace tips),
and a fine pair of yellow kid gloves." Now tell me whither
the ascendancy of spats? the suzerainty of the zoot suit?
"Whither"? "Sartorialness"? There are no vows
of faithfulness from fashion.
The neck ruff. And the tight, long (often
fringed) sheath of a flapper's dress, that makes my manhood
arise from its shameful slumber. Yowch: *did* I write that? What
limbo held the poetry of John Donne all those hundreds of years,
before the tastes of the twentieth century lifted it
out of its midden dump, and back into the light
of an empathetic reconsideration? What
a student called, just yesterday, "the zeitgeese"
weren't flying along with Donne . . . then, later (now)
they were (are). Not the six-inch-diameter hot-pink
polka dots on the vinyl skirts of the '70s. Not
Martin Van Buren's grand beaver-fur hat. Time

gargles with these, with *us,* and spits it out.
With *us!* Those sweet-cheeked punk-rock women wearing
—and (oh so lissomely) often *not* wearing—
"the vinyl skirts of the '70s" . . . where,
as Villon, in his famous ballad asks us, *are* the snows
of yesteryear? "Lissomely"?—brother, you gotta be kidding, right?
Time that knackers us heartlessly on its chop block.
"Knackers"? Knickers. Pinafores. Bustles. Here's one: "Dungarees."
The clothes of yesteryear: -wear; where? We're
gleaming earrings Time admires extravagantly for a night,
goes ooh, goes wow, then leaves behind
in the creased-up sheets or on the edge of the sink
at noon-sharp checkout. There, by the stand
with the barrister's wig and the tortoiseshell-inlay buttonhook.
"Midden dump"? "Clit ring"? "Porkpie hat"? Or:
"famous ballad"? Huh? Who? Surely to a vein of gneiss,
the line between "cultural style" and "fad"
(as when Tahiti's an island but England a continent) is dew
in the touch of the rosy-fingered dawn, a thing
I can't believe I wrote, and *barely* a "thing": it's disappearing
even now into the afternoon light. "When eighteenth-century
London bookseller James Lackington was a young man,"
writes Anne Fadiman, "his wife sent him out on Christmas Eve
with half a crown—all they had—to buy Christmas dinner."
He returned with a book, Young's *Night Thoughts.* "I think
I have acted wisely. Should we live fifty years longer,
we shall have the *Night Thoughts* to feast upon." —A story
that stirs the blood of the biblio-idiot who lives in me and drools
for gilded leather spines, but *whoooa,* have you ever
tried to read that book?—the zeitgeese zoomed on down
and pecked it to death a few cultural styles ago,
oh Time that sent its insidious basilisks into my mother's lungs,
oh Time in your *obi,* Time below your masses of pompadour hair,

come take me, I'm open, I'm yours, I want to be undone
like a row of real whalebone corset stays
and ravished. "Stirs the blood"?—*I* wrote this? Actually,
no, I wish that Time would leave me alone, immutable, here
with the "trilby" and "derby" and "bloomers" and "hoop skirt" and
speaking of Time, "men's moleskin vest
with oxblood leather-trim fob pocket: LASTS A LIFETIME!",
the river, the geese overhead.

Space and Time

"You Might Notice Blood in Your Urine for a Couple of Weeks" /
& Scenes from the American Revolution ⁓

I was like a taster that the kings use;
if the grapes are fatal, the taster dies.
And so all of my male friends my age
were almost as anxious waiting
for the report on my prostate biopsy
as I was. I was their crystal ball,
their tea leaves, I was the lure for an unguessable catch.
"What is it like?" (Not that they ever asked this
so forthrightly.) How does it feel, in the fogs and cumulonimbus
of the land of indeterminacy?
And my answer included fear of course but, more than that,
a greed for even the beauty of the scantest bead
of spray-on damp
bejeweling the florets of broccoli at the salad bar
as they refuse to wilt, for even a single lash
that fringed my wife's shut eye and fed in her sleep
on its own minute allotment of oils . . . I wouldn't yield
any portion of these to oblivion, *nothing*
too subepidermal or superlunary
for my newfound and possibly short-lived care,
and when these friends of mine were going hormonally gaga
over a stripper's slinky, fleshy pleats and impeccable smoothness,
I could have wept for staring at nothing
more articulate and lovely than the way
the shadows under her breasts reminded me of the vowels
under Hebrew and Arabic consonants—I wouldn't overlook a single
calorie of exuded human warmth. One night I bit a book
to see my teethmarks, to remind me I had saliva and will,
and out of a taste for the paper itself. The book was *Patriots*
(A. J. Langguth). In chapter 17, a troop of colonial soldiers suffers
the frozen swamps and brambled forests of the march up to Quebec.
They lose their rations. They boil their moccasins for soup.
When those are gone, they wrap their bleeding feet in flour bags,

and continue. They can't *not* continue on, or hug the last
bedraggled, shitty, wonderful shred of themselves to themselves.
They kill the captain's great black slobbery dog
and eat everything including its guts, then gather the bones
and pound them to dust and brew a greenish broth of that.
They dole this out like a fine Madeira wine
and smack their lips and swirl their tongues.
Because they won't let go.
Because they still have lips and tongues.

A woman is darning a petticoat.
Outside her window it's April 18, 1775,
and the very air tonight is heavier
and charged, as if the revolution announces its close approach
the way a storm would . . . so the boughs of trees seem dense
with whispering thought like rows of brains, and the dirt
stirs out of its ease in ways that alarm the chickens from sleep.
Buckshot is being stored up; swanshot; grapeshot.
This is the night that Paul Revere sets down
the client's teeth he's carving out of a diced-down hippopotamus tusk;
his mission is to row across the Charles, undetected
by a hulking British man-of-war, the *Somerset,*
and deliver a warning to Hancock and Adams in Lexington.
Empire! Liberty! Carnage!—huge ideas encumber the night.
But we can't fault this woman for smaller attention,
to her garment and its rip. Her frugal life.
Her dainty fingers that we can imagine just as readily
stroking a lover's hair, some young man done for the day
at the barrel-maker's and hurrying up her stairs
for the pleasureful rumpus that momentarily outweighs
even a memory of the bundles of staves on his shoulders.
As she stitches, she's naked: a breeze is an intimate
touch she's always appreciated. And when she's finished

mending it, she slips back into the petticoat: the air by now
is too cool, and she draws the curtain shut, and sits here,
quietly enjoying the heat of her body as it doubles back
upon itself, deliciously, under her ruffles. I would like to think
that this is an implicit understanding of how all too soon
all flesh is too, too cool: and any tiniest resistance is a victory
against that. By the morning, Deacon Hayes would be dead,
killed by a British shot as he reloaded his musket.
And old Jonas Parker: dead. And a wounded British soldier
—his head was split to the brain-meat by a Massachusetts boy
who came upon him with a tomahawk. Altogether,
forty-nine American bodies cooling in the dawn sun, and
(the long guns used to hunt duck proved effective) seventy-three
of the British infantrymen. What *would* I say
if my long week of impatiently waiting a lab report were spent
back there, in gathering intelligence for communiqués
snuck forward to the future? I don't know; although
I'm picturing my friends around the amber glow
of a pitcher of beer in bar light, when it suddenly
and mysteriously pours sound forth, like a radio,
and a gargle of homilies interrupts their boozey talk:
Love every stitch. Remember every thread. And so they startle;
then shrug; and go on joking. In any case, I'm not there.
Paul Revere is there. In his worry and haste,
he's neglected to bring the cloths that he normally uses
to muffle the plash of his oars. But luckily,
one of the young men who'd been appointed to accompany him
on this clandestine launch—a slim, wisecracking
barrel-maker's assistant—leads them to his sweetheart's house
and whistles below her window. When she learns the problem,
she removes her petticoat and flings it, as she might a kiss,
to the deepening chill of the night air. A. J. Langguth:
"The flannel was still warm when it was passed to Paul Revere."

The Spices ⁓

No, it's not "the painting"—not the *noun* of it—
that serves now to remind her of her day.
In fact the scene in its frame, the scene in all its dense, strategic
counterpoints of hue and shape, presents
a sense of caution and control. It's the *verb,*
the "act" of "painting": sensing how, originally,
the dog was only half a dog, a shaky and hesitant
tan-gray blur, the oils of its body puddling
into the neighboring oils of the herring vendor's cart, which
also only was a fragment of itself, a sort of iffy
fetal version of a cart, before the painter's frantic hand was off
to scribble in a patch of far horizon, and up
to a glaringly loud, then scratched out, then replenished,
tentative, tilting, hyperbolic, crammed-full night sky

. . . *that's* her day, her way-past-any-sane-control day,
which indeed began with a dog, a dowdy terrier from out
of the cloudy blue, which she ran over with an ugly, endless
crunch, and stopped to cuddle, and rush to the only nearby
vet she knew of, who happened to be her ex, and *that* began
an afternoon of sex and quick regret Shakespearian
in its thundering, and SWAT team in its overall effect.
As if it isn't enough her son is still a barnacle
attached to a dialysis machine; as if it's not enough
the evening news is terror bomb, mob rule, red tide,
brown recluse. Didn't her college physics tell her
it's an undependable laissez-faire of energy and emptiness
around us, in us—*is* us? So no wonder
we find her alternately shivering like a sick child tonight

and ordering the spices on her kitchen shelf, repeatedly,
until the sunrise stops her at an arbitrary moment in the middle
of arranging them according to a system of chromatic values: *now,*
at last, she can open herself to sleep and dream
of patterns that we trust exist, which balance out the chaos
we would otherwise be beckoned to explore
until we drown. No wonder a fifteenth-century bishop duly tabulated
the number of fallen angels—one-hundred-thirty-three-million,
three-hundred-and-six-thousand, six-hundred-sixty-eight.
There are twenty-eight angels "ruling the twenty-eight serial mansions
of the moon," and we can list these lunar radiances by day of month
or alphabetically starting with Abdízuel (Tágriel last).
Nine hundred thousand insect species . . . we need each of these
Linnaean labels, faced with such macabretude. No wonder

this poem relies on a pattern of fourteen lines. But enough
about me. It's morning in a village in the Netherlands
in the fifteenth century. Even this early in Europe's sorrowful history
of the plague, an anxious father is alert enough
about an infant daughter's spotted chest to spend
the day in seeking out whatever rituals or poultices
could cure her . . . first a midwife, then a leecher,
then the amulets man, the sweet-but-syphilitic priest,
the seller of saintly knucklebones, an herb-witch . . . anybody
who might let him play the dice of chance
in favor of his child. And he feels like some mad,
zigzagging die himself, that's cast about the village
in a game of drunken rules. At last, it's dusk,
he rests a moment near the herring vendor's cart,

and in an almost painterly veil of lavender light he sees
a dog lick at its own fresh tan-gray splotch of vomit
—something like crude parody of a swan and its reflections. So
the stench of day's-end fish and worse still irritates
his mind when he arrives home, checks the crib, then starts
to set out thimble portions of the rare, imported cinnamon,
nutmeg, and ginger he dearly purchased: for the herb-witch promised
these exotic fragrances would keep all plague at bay.
He arranges and rearranges them scrupulously around the crib.
At least for now he's done all he can. At least
he feels a structure is at work on his behalf. He steps
outside—the stars are beautiful and small. He used to sail,
once: he knows them like friends. And look: a brand-new moon
so slim and sharp, you could use it to pick your teeth.

Scenes from the Next Life

At other times, an unwrapped mummy held a surprise: parts of animal skeletons, which were mingled with the human remains.

This was the way I served the Pharaoh, God of the Two Lands,
this was how I provided the God a service for all of my days
in his protection: I was keeper of one of the houses
where the soldiers and the overseers would come for their beer
at the end of a shift, when the Boat of the Sun descended
into the nether part of its journey. As they labored
in the hard press of the light, I stayed inside, and cared
for the rough clay cups and the customary onions.
As they broke themselves, and healed, and toughened,
laboring with rock, with war, with the chase, I grew
increasingly soft: my belly, like a ball of paste, could take
a seal-imprint. I was proud of this, I added to it
with lotions, I was a lotus in dew. And then I died,
and awoke in this skin you could thump on like a casket.

This is how much time is between us: you
believe in a flexible, self-willed destiny. Yes, and whenever
the animal rises up in you, it's only in a dream, and not
as a blood tie, not as your deity finally
taking you into its own beast fist. For me. . . . How,
you may ask, did I afford my luxurious lotions
—and the pendant-eyes of lapis with which I purchased love
from the temple girls? It was easy: I watered the beer.
I watched for customers who dozed, I filched their pouches,
or better, I had the girls do it. And over the days,
the many days, what you would call my heart became
a tooth; my heart became a chill, acidic hunger;
a belly; a jar of sour green need; a stone of a heart.
And after I died, they gave me the breast of the crocodile.

*For example, the wing of an ibis was found
attached to a young boy's shoulder.*

I was told when in school that in death, at last,
we know everything. I know about you: your thunder-ships
that travel through the sky, your beginning ability to sculpt
your future generations. I know about the crocodile man.
But I will never understand what it was,
in the mind of that one artisan in the necropolis shops
who went to a storeroom, came back out with this exquisite
wrongness, and jumbled it into my body literally
forever. Maybe he was lazy; drunk; rebellious; or
—*anything,* I couldn't *start* to guess behind this joke
or cruelty or error. Maybe he was lame, and wanted to send
a kindred spirit into the light beyond the tomb,
so fashioned his ideal cousin, and then announced
there! represent me.

I could say that I'm a map of what we were—a map of *one* thing
that we were—before we were human; just as I'm a premonition
of Judaeo-Christian heaven: something wingéd. All of that,
however, is far too grand. I'm just a boy, a boy of ten,
who only made it part-way to a man: and so is only, now,
part-this, part-that, in the Fields and Halls of Eternity.
Look: one side of me can rise!—a little. And then
it turns into merely a shrug. To be half a bird is to be
completely a monster. Even so, I love to feel this delicate
comb of bone—that I've been given instead of an arm—
accept the rush of evening air; and if I lift it then,
I can be played on like a harp. If I don't know
the euphoria of flight itself, at least
I know the quieter joy of its blueprint.

The Views

Their party—a various dozen of them, a vicar,
a tough young streetjack, a lady's waiting maid, etc.—
had been kidnapped from the ferry by a raiding ship,
and *that* was attacked by enemy cannon, and then
their adventures *really* began. It's dawn now,
and they wake on the other side of a day of long trek
through the villages of this mountainous, alien land.
They're in an abandoned plaza. Overnight, a number
of their belongings have disappeared: some purses, food bags.
In the nearer vista, the ruin of a temple spills the morning
light like burning brandy over its marble lip. *The world
is a large and marvelous place,* someone is thinking reverently,
strange, and visibly miracled. One slaps his pocket: wallet gone.
Jezusfukkinchrist, he says, *the same old story wherever you go.*

Thread ⁓

. . . the days we now remember only in poetry and song.

⁓ Sean Russell

The god is weakening.
(Undiluted belief is the blood of a god,
and the people's belief is weakening.)
Look: already, he lifts his hand
and sees its once definitively hard-edged shape
is sleet, is only sweater-fuzz
adrift in the sky like a nebula.
The god is growing less than limber,
less than a proper deific opaque—remember how the terror
and the solace he inspired were
as real as a paving stone? The priesthood, now . . .
and that ritual with the adolescent girls in gowns of flowers . . .
their heart isn't in it. Only once or twice
a year does a column of offering-smoke ascend, and this
the god pulls like a great rope up from Earth,
his muscles toughening to the task . . . a rope like one
that bears a bucket from the deepness of a well,
and in its circle of heavily mineral water the god can see
his face: it trembles slightly when the water does,
but still it's his face.

⁓

That rope . . . let's say for people (as much as for gods),
for *us* . . . we won't let go. We won't give up
that thread-of-remaining-attached-to-what-we-once-were.
("Won't"?—or "can't"? It's not as if
the newer, airy upper regions of our brain *can* snip
their anchoring, dank stem away, and so float
in the lucid juice of pure thought for eternity, no
—not even if they want to, and they don't.

It's something like the way the current tribal elders
make their somber, monthly pilgrimage to the burial grounds
of the ancestor-ones: and there, with the various
singsong lists of formulaic compliments, and
the wax-plugged jars of fish mush and casava beer
[what we might call a "consultation fee"], they
seek the wisdom of their forebears, on a whole
agenda of topical woes: so does
our neocortex sometimes travel down the dark
for the advice of its precursor).

Yes, and so the Husband-Daddy—when
it's late, and he's steeped deep in a nostalgic funk,
and bone-weary again—spends
furtive, hazy moments slowly paging through
an album of his high school soccer glories
(yowza, *this* one in the locker room: *whoa,* check out his abs!),
the way that Mommy-Wife still owns those photos
of her party-hearty nights when she could swing
a derriere that left the street a mess of skidmarks.

"When I take Cale fishing," Gil says—Cale's
six—"it's like . . . *my* father took *me* fishing . . . crappie,
bluegill . . . and this fishing line—" he points
at a snapshot "—keeps us, you know, tied
to a tradition. It's not so much we cast
the hook out; it's . . . we cast *ourselves* back in time."
"How far?" I idly ask, just to make conversation.
He points me to the picture again: Cale's
using both hands to display a fish as long as his leg,
a gnarl-faced old battlebear of a thing,

goon-lipped and whiskery. "It's just one wart and an overbite
short of being my greatgrandpa Amos."

     ~

"Satellite images show a massive plume of sand
swirled out of the Sahara, reaching Britain
on February 13th. Foot-and-mouth disease
has a seven-day incubation period, and the UK's
epidemic began on February 20th."
                                   There *are* bonds
of such enormity, they're spread to a thinness
past our normal vision; still, they play our lives
like the stringing on marionettes.
                                 Just ask
that man in Sweden, who donated sperm
"so a lesbian couple—friends of his—
could have three children": now the couple has split,
and "the Swedish court said that because the man is provably
the biological father, he's obliged to pay monthly child support."
Holy moley.
                There *are* chains of such exquisite fastening,
they hold a heart the way
the oolong's held fast in its silver, armorial tea ball.
Everywhere: tethering.
                    The height of a bird
above the Earth is measurable by the size
of its shadow; once the shadow disappears
completely—once the allegiance finally snaps—
the sky takes over.

     ~

Cale was one, and held up a stone to his father
for clarification. "Stone," said Gil, and Cale

was satisfied: he was "Cale," this was "Stone."
He lifted up another. "Stone," said Gil.
"No, *this* one!" "Right: stone," said Gil. *"No! No!"*
—not wanting a *class* of objects; holding,
holding dearly to the notion of individual name.
It may have been a way of loving his own uniqueness.
Not "boy," but "Cale." Clinging to that Cale-thread.

Their daughter's asleep, and Mommy and Daddy
have a little wine buzz, so are viewing the fuzzy video
of their senior prom—the ballroom dance
itself, and then some astigmatic footage of the party
("party"?—just say "sex") on the beach. In a way,
this parallels the gesture I heard made today
when I joined, from curiosity, a walking tour
by the Downtown Renovation Project membership.
This building, here, was slated for demolition. Over there,
that building, its dangerous cornicework had to come down.
But *this, here!*—and an elderly woman pointed with affection
at a frieze of inch-square tiles, seafoam green and tan
with a kind of diner-deco kick, that ran
below a row of glass-brick inlay for the length of a block.
"This stays. *This stays*. Because it's a nerve
directly connecting back to this city's history
in the 1930s and '40s." Then she stopped; and added:
"A better time." Which is why, of course,
I'm thinking about the look in the eyes of that couple
—a look of loss, but also of pride in what
was lost. *There,* see?—this scene
in the waves! That laughter! They had
. . . well, they had the bodies of gods.

And their kid they sung asleep about an hour ago?
—is curled up, peacefully sucking her thumb:
the mouth itself, independent of brain,
remembering its time at the nipple.
Nor do the parents—cunnilingus; fellatio—relinquish that
fulfillment.
        And the words on the computer screen
remember their life on paper; as the letters of the words
on paper still contain—when we know how to look—
their earliest, literal life as objects: head of an ox; jar;
doorposts and a lintel.
        Some rag paper
in the early twentieth century was manufactured
using strips of winding-cloth off mummies; what
long linkage to the pantheons of ancient Egypt
—ibis-headed, jackal-headed, crocodile-headed—were intact
inside the atoms of the headlines of the daily news
in Pittsburgh and Schenectady?
        Let's say
the god looks down to track the image of himself
on the coins of the people, over generations. First
a clear, imposing, sternly lineated figure
—which was copied, just one wobble at a time,
into an abstract scribble. Later—maybe centuries,
but only a blink to a god—the new designers of coins
attempt to read a literal shape back into this mess,
a lion in front of a flaming tree, or two cranes
flying over a hill, or a water pitcher:
not the god, it isn't the god at all, and yet
(he clings to this like a life preserver)
some of the god's creations.

One day Gil bent down to pick a toy of Cale's off the floor
and when he stood up, he was blind in one eye.
Like that—*a snap*—from out of nowhere,
no pain, no forewarning: completely blind in one eye.
A lodged clot. Medication is theoretically prohibiting
new clots from ever forming, but as for the dead eye
—all they can do is wait, is "wait and see," as Gil
ironically puts it. And he says, "By now, my brain
is accommodated to one-eye vision. I read, I drive.
There's a little difference; not much. I mean, I miss
the old life, but I'm still me." They say every
—what? is it seven years? I think so—we're entirely
new cells: *entirely,* nerve sheath, nose, and sphincter.
Are we us? Are we *another* us? "There's a fantasy I have,"
says Gil—a long, long cord, and
at its farther end, very tiny, is Gil's own former
full-sight self. Hand over hand, Gil pulls his way
along that lifeline, back to his past. At the same time,
hand over hand, the other figure moves closer,
into its future. Both of them are the astronaut.
Both of them are the mother ship.

OUT-OF-THE-BODY TRAVEL

Some Ways

My friend Judith dreamed a frightening dream.
    "I was driving a car, but I couldn't
control it. I couldn't stop it either.
I was weaving around in these great and dangerous
arcs: it was really terrifying."
    "And then?"
She laughs:
    "I looked down and saw I was naked. And
I said to myself, 'Honey, this
is only a dream.' Well it was,
so I woke up."

There are many ways the conscious self
returns. In stories of out-of-body experience,
the "astral awareness" sometimes shinnies
laboriously along its connective tendril,
an Alpine-mountaineer-of-a-spirit.
Sometimes, though: the ease of a high pop
dropping cleanly into its very solid smack with the mitt.

In the mingling that followed my poetry reading
in Salisbury, Maryland, a seventy-year-old woman,
Betty Prue, told me "too much emotion" often made her
"leave [her]self," and as I started to shape a request
for examples, her eyeballs emptied out
like two bar stools at closing time, and she fell
to the floor in a seizure. She shook,
which was horrible. But then the shaking left too,
and the remnant emptiness was even worse;
the shudders, at least, had been *something*.

It can come back with the drama of a moon shot
shedding tons of on-fire debris across the ocean,
it can come back like the family car
that floats into place in the garage as if
predestined from the moment of Creation: *good car,*
good car. When my wife wakes up
in the morning, she raises one arm,
then the other, and seems to me to be studying
each hand with a scrutiny that's first amazed
the hand is there at all, and then is relieved at the hand's
increasing familiarity, like siblings
reunited after years. I can see her self return to herself
in separate, continuous clumps
—the whole line of cows at last back in their fold.

And it would be correct to say "the eyelids
fluttered." It would be correct enough
to say how it began that way. And yet we knew
before the flutter made itself apparent
on her shut eyes—and before the awful zero
of her face regained a few tenths of its former definition—
that whatever we call "being" had retraced its path
and entered Betty Prue again: who, for a while,
hadn't "been," in any form
except for shallow breath itself. The rescue folk
arrived with their stretcher and canisters, and we worked
hard to convince Ms. Pure to go with them
to ER, but she wouldn't yield: "I can drive
myself home." But what if this happens again,
behind the wheel? She shook her head unbudgeably:
as if stating a universal truth:

"Driving. Isn't. Emotion."
And, well . . . there was no arguing with that.

⁓

It happens as many ways as there's us.
The image I prefer is simply the end
of an ordinary day, when the colors are deep,
and we stand outside, and silently, as one,
the shadows are called back into our bodies.

The Invisible World

A little bit of mass is worth an awful lot of energy. For example, one gram of matter, converted into electricity, could power an entire city for several days.

⁓ Paul Davies

This might explain ghosts, or ESP: the stuff of us is worth more
in the invisible world, as a source of fuel. It surely explains
why the universe is a field of here-then-not-here laws
and nano-warp and slant, half-state existences that's larger
than all of its solids combined; and why our moods
are a turbulent current the body can rarely swim against.
Even in sleep, the bonds in the brain are fire the size
of a galaxy's suns. Even in death, the brain is not a stone:
it hums in the earth, it does its ceaseless isometrics in the bellies
of dismantler-beetles. A *stone* is not a stone: it's the moon;
or at least it's a moon-equivalency, in its subatomic potential.
And the moon?—is seducing the ocean into cresting higher,
out of itself. And the land?—it could explode from the ocean's
teasing it, for night after night, with the foam hem of her flamenco dress.

Hoverers

he lost her / she left him /
so many ways to say it

The day outside is mizzly, and inside—I mean
inside—the day is mizzly too: the opium
creates a friendly fog in the brambles of Coleridge's brain,
and in this biochemical possibility-state, the minarets
of Xanadu take shape, "from two to three hundred lines,"
and the—*Hallooo,* the famous intrusive "person
on business from Porlock." So he lost the poem.
The poem of fog dispersed like fog. It left him.
What we have now is Coleridge fervently pressing the cool
of the crystal inkwell to his brow, as if to wake
his inner eye, and walking circles through the room
as if this purely physical repetition might somehow
call forth repeated vision. Circling. Think of the birds
that migrated back to Atlantis, circling the empty sea.

driving around her block all night / he counted 317 times /
& still the windows dark / & still the sign FOR SALE

sees bees—a note for a poem, that intervening time has since
consigned to vapor. Now it's one of the many floating ghosts
outnumbering the living. They return, and stir the air
like blurry spoons above the sites of their unfinished business.
Every culture has its version of these hoverers; as every individual
has a weather map of spirals that are one part of the thoughtosphere
over the mind: dead loves, abandoned dreams . . . .
And so the pain, or maybe even a maze of fevered kisses,
is a ghost dance that revisits the stump

of an amputated leg. And in the days
of my recent sorrow, when they said I was "distracted" . . .
from the snapping of my neural links, a mist arose,
an ultrasubtle rosin, that followed me everywhere
with its gossamer tugs, imploring.

he would eat her for hours / he couldn't leave
the gates from which we enter this life

She'd left him; if being companionable is an accurate measure
of marital success . . . why then, she'd left him
though she sat right there at the window shelling garden peas,
as he'd left *her*. Yet even miles away now,
alpenstocking over a neighbor's nettled meadow,
Coleridge obsessively thinks of their earliest days together,
Sarah undoing her chignon and the sudden sun in it
like a waterfall. . . . He sees that someone's relocated
the beehive at the base of Fuller's Hill by a couple of yards,
and that the bees—this isn't unusual—have come back
from their foraging to buzz inside the vacated space.
It's beautiful, in its hopeless way, and Coleridge halts
for an hour or more: they won't stop making the tight invisible
coils of a hive in the air.

Called from Out of the Lines of Your Life ~~~~

1.

A clear way to begin
would be with a man on a country road
in rising sun—a man as plain as day,
and certainly as plain as *this*
as-yet-unsullied dawn.
A man—or let's say a protagonist—as clear
to himself and to us as if fresh
from the stamp of a cookie cutter. Now
let's suppose the swales at the side of the road
are thick in a batting of morning fog,
and let's suppose the man skips in and out
of this obscurement—he . . . *envagues* himself,
let's say. He raises his hand
and there isn't a "hand," not if by hand we mean
an outlined thing. He raises his voice,
he says his name—or maybe he says
her name. On the road, a said name means a person.
In the swales, a name is only a part of the fog.
Now let's suppose the fog
is *in* the person, let's suppose that
that's what I've been talking about.

2.

Another way to say it would be Eloise and Daniel; even now they're shuffling into
view, in a dishabille of terry cloth, their arms around each other in such a basic, lucid
visual cue, they could serve as an international symbol, LOVE, or the sign on a yellow
highway marker, CAUTION: LOVERS CROSSING. It's good to give them names,
to see this cliché state-of-being from the songs and the poems and the greeting cards
solidified, made immanent and specific, in these two adult shapes and their physical
declaration of mutual care.

Perhaps it's especially affecting because these aren't kids—her hair is gray, and his is too sparse for assigning a color at all—and still they're dreamy and rapt "like kids." They walk in an eloquent silence, into his room, and they close its door on the world, and then get down to the dizzily pleasureful, fleshy business of *their* insular world. And *then?* . . .

An attendant opens the door. They keep all doors unlocked at Oak Grove Home for Special Residence—what we would have called, in the dark ages forty years gone now, when we bundled Grandpa Louie away to the cotton smocks and mousily gray broths of his new (and final) existence, an "old people's home." The issue of privacy wasn't clear then and isn't clearer now, in part because the legal and ethical definitions of self-reliance in senility aren't clear. We easily tweezed him off the couch like an unwanted hair from a lip, and set him on what seemed like permanent hallway display in the pea green linoleum deeps of that drably gothic building.

You can imagine the small, sad subsequence: the immediate internly hubbub, Eloise ungently removed from the scene of her amorous entanglement (it's prima facie assumed that Daniel's stubbornly coerced her), the two of them relocated to separate wings of their ward. And *then?* . . . As you guessed, they psychologically dwindle from now on (she'll be dead in slightly over a year, of a "failure to thrive"), their regimen of the psychotropic Mellaril won't help (in fact he'll lose some motor control of his tongue as a side effect), the whole concerted battalion of institutional diversions and counselings . . . nothing helps, the one thing that would heal is unallowed, is only a peg, a marble, lost in the overriding miasma of medical terminology.

Everything's seemingly lost from a clear grasp. Eloise and Daniel believe they're wife and husband—but Daniel is married to someone else, someone outside Oak Grove he hasn't seen or remembered for three years. Orderlies believe they have the contractual right to enter a resident's room at will (or whim)—but written policy only addresses this great question in the sloshiest of language. Edges everywhere soften and oh so leisurely effervesce from sight. . . .

. . . the same bevapored shapelessness and floating that, if swiveled crosswise some degrees and squinted at, becomes what we call *reverie* or *rumination*. Out of this slurred mindscape, Einstein saw the multidimensional round of the universe the way *we* would an orange on a linen, and Dickinson understood the travel of the light of the sun to its culminant highlighting bulge on the breast of a gull in flight.

Last night my friend Di's mother, eighty-seven, filled the doldrums air of her golden-agers apartment complex, shrieking oaths (and lung-blood) to the effect that her firstborn *hadn't* died of natural complications in the hospital's postpartum ward—no, she'd smothered him, she'd pressed the pillow into his mewling, rubicund face.

It's nonsense of course—there were staff and family witnesses at the moment that his hooked-up breath caved in. But her sincerity is real, and if the spiked-out fright-wig hair and unkempt robes of the hokier moments in Greek tragedy—its pat- and mat- and fratricides— are viable components of confession, her stentorian disclosure in the third-to-fourth-floor stairwell is persuasive indeed.

Sixty years of an infant's body accumulating waves of fact-distorting pall.

Yet out of a not-dissimilar years-long cloudiness, someone's "inner eye" retrieves, intact, the image of those daffodils "beside the lake" that, thronging there, "outdid the sparkling waves in glee"—a solace for the introspective Wordsworth, yielded up from an interior murk as if plucked in its bright entirety from the bottom of an oystermonger's barrel.

"A neighbor led her back up the stairs to her apartment. When I got there—how can I put it? She looked no more *complete* to me than car exhaust."

There are far too many versions of this fog, to think we *won't* be lost inside it (or not have it lost in us), a watercolor left out overnight in rain, a pat of rouge sneezed from its compact.

3.

A man is hammering.
Each hard arc of hammer through the June air
is an erasure of detail
—much as the hummingbird's wing-blur
generalizes the space it exists in

(only, sized now to the force
of being human). All morning: hammering,
with the quick precision, the matter-of-fact
intensity, that might have gone
into banging the Argo together, or the Ark,

although this laundered chambray shirt
a daughter patched with one of the sew-on
rainbow appliqués out of her trinket drawer,
this sky this afternoon and no other, this
sky with its mulletbone clouds . . . these

fight to keep the scene from blearing
into schema, these don't want to hear
the murmurrings of gods, don't want
to fix this man on a strand
of the web of history—no,

his name is Daniel, his wife is Sydney Rae,
the faded red-&-yellow label on the oblong inner lid
of his utility box says Trust-Tool, and the trellis
he's completing is to rung the upward travel
of a climbing rose called Dixie Traveler, that

rose and no other, these specific and undeniable
lives and their razor-edged ideas and
no others, no-isms, -ologies, no wavering
of process or of outcome, and no nightly news
that was also the news in Ur and Carthage and Ilium.

4.

In Turner it's grandiloquent—those massive banked-up slopes of rolled-in ocean fog, their rich sfumato moving with the implacable gait of a glacier; or Thames-fog, riding like a dirty risen cream on the skin of the barely there river; or smoke of course—in *Burning of the Houses of Parliament* (1835), the nearly incandescent yellows of that conflagration shade into roils of purple and hazy grays that are simply, purely "air and atmosphere and infinite spaces . . . in paint" (Paul Johnson, *The Birth of the Modern*).

Kenneth Clark reminds us that "for centuries objects were thought to be real because they were solid . . . and all respectable art aimed at defining this solidity." Turner's work—sometimes his seascapes look like paint applied directly onto breath—becomes "entirely," says Clark, "a new approach." John Gilbert astoundedly witnesses Turner "absorbed. . . . He had a large palette, nothing on it but a huge lump of flake-white: he had two or three biggish hog-tools to work with, and with these he was driving the white into all the hollows and every part of the surface."

This newness is easily seen, comparing William Frith's railroad station (1862) with Monet's ascendantly insubstantial series on St. Lazare (about 1877). According to Robert Harbison, "Frith crowds the canvas with separate bits: sweepers cleaning, children lost, fond farewells, high life, low life, age, infancy, spectacle; but the most intriguing parts of Monet's scenes are above eye level, in the magical smoke suspended in its arbitrariness forever . . . an etherealizing."

Turner had been capturing this industrial smear for decades already—his *Rain, Steam, Speed* is a brilliantly scumbled-up mix of atmospheric effects and a locomotive's blending-in huffs. It's 1820. England is first creating its mantle of manufactory char, and Turner is one of its first great witnesses. He's seen the Glasgow soda works (the largest chemical factory then in the world), its endless armadas of hydrochloric-acid gas afloat on high.

It's such a sky-wide dinge beneath which Wordsworth loses himself in bemoaning that "The world is too much with us." (How to keep intact a viable image of daffodils, in days of such increasing obfuscation?)

How to keep intact. . . . These are, of course, also the glory days of Empire. How to retain the sense of one's cultural self in the midst of all of those mitigating hottentot-esque wastes? Amidst sarong and sari and drumbeat-down-your-bop-bone, how to keep up a true dose of starch in one's staunch?

Mountstuart Elphinestone served the Crown in various Indian Residencies, including Benares and Poona. "We rise at four and read Sophocles, generally about 200 lines. . . . After breakfast business usually prevents our beginning Xenophon, till eleven; we then read 20 or 30 pages, eat a sandwich and read separately—I Tacitus and the books on the French Revolution till two; and then we read Grotius until evening."

As Harbison richly puts it, "The English secret was not an ability to cast off home, but rather to carry it along tortoiselike."

Or else—? You "went bush," you "went native," you were called from out of the lines of your life by hoodoo flute, by hammock-sway, by juice of the kiwi and mango. You were abstracted into the furnacey air and the over-resplendent flora. You became the id-less element of a continent.

Isn't this one view of Paul Gauguin, fleeing what he called "filthy Europe" in 1891? He begins: "On the eighth of June, during the night, after a sixty-three days' voyage, sixty-three days of feverish expectancy, we perceived strange fires, moving in zigzags on the sea. From the somber sky a black cone with indentations became disengaged.

"We turned Morea and had Tahiti before us."

And later: "All this drunkeness of lights and perfumes with its enchantment and mystery. The fever throbbed in my temples, and my knees shook."

Mystery. . . . Fifteenth-century Chinese poet-painter Shen Chou gives us, in his *Poet on a Cliff-top,* a figure facing into Nothingness like a dish antenna tuned to Nothing's voice. "White clouds like a belt / encircle the mountain's waist / A stone ledge flying into space. . . ." The figure looks like a compilation of particles soon to evaporate into a flimmery osmosis with the Beyond.

Yes: it will seek us out, wherever we are, no matter the weight of our rootedness. It will issue its invitation. There's a 1960 Japanese schlockola sci-fi flick, *The Human Vapor,* about, says Michael Barson, "a man who can turn himself into mist" by relying on "power siphoned from the stars." He *becomes*—so *always was,* in chemical poten-tial—a mist. The poster: "Born of Woman—Re-Created by Outer Space!"

5.

It happens,
then it doesn't h

—erased,

out of forgetfulness
perhaps, or simply out of last night's chilliness
billowing up at the touch of the sun.
Let's say a man
somewhere is walking casually through these vales
/veils/

let's say: Daniel. Or is it
a woman? let's say Elo

—another waft of obscurement.
In such milky indeterminacy
it could be, why not?—Wordsworth

in a Grasmere dawn: "Wordsworth walked
continually," Clark tells us, and "thought nothing
of walking sixteen miles after dinner
to post a letter." Here he is now

—if it's him, a ghost of a shape
in a ghost of a landscape,

looking for something . . . sublimity?
some unbroken thread through the days,
through the ooze, the soup, the goop,
the whatnot. Now he bends

to . . . *something:* after all this time,
a daffo—?

—no, a *peg,* a *marble,* from so long ago

as my own second section.* Let's say

that he could even *be* the writer or
the reader of this poem.

_____

* ". . . a peg, a marble, lost in the overriding miasma of medical terminology."

6.

Turner's sight eventually was cataracted: does this account, in part, for the heady brume of his later paintings? Cézanne was severely myopic. And of course that last emphatic beauty of the stricken Monet: it's exactly that line where "vision" fails, and "visionary" soaringly takes over. In his waterlilies series, the flowers yield themselves to the painterly matrix like unshelled yolks, expanding in his water, mixing proteanly, becoming what the primary colors dream of when the lights go out: their spiritualsexual shading-off into a blendworld of pastels.

Is this how Eloise sees Daniel?—as a moment of beauty, late in her life, *created by* the blear. In any case, once they're separated, she sinks back into her usual stupor—softly, like a globule of butter reversing itself, back into the uniform cream.

We will all know our version of this. "Over one-and-a-half *million* Americans currently live in nursing homes"; of these, about 60 percent are diagnosed to show some degree of dementia. Literally or symbolically, we will all be subsumed into these statistics. Verily—we will all trace a forefinger over the inner wall of our own skulls, to see it tipped with the ashy by-products of flux and otherness. A friend sends me a handwritten letter: he feels "so confirmed in [his] new marriage." Or did he write "confined"? I can't tell. Maybe he can't tell. Maybe it's both things, maybe it's many compounded nothings, maybe particle and wave are switching partners on the dance floor in us every second, and this is the flickering subtext that we carry into our outer lives. O, we will all rise from the asphalt like heat waves, into the realm of the imprecise.

Athena McLean, a cultural anthropologist applying fieldwork theory to "a dementia unit," provides this working definition of "cognitive capacity": "a person's awareness of his surroundings and identity, and his ability to reason." (Daniel: low. Eloise: low.) "Nursing homes, in deciding how seriously to take a resident's desires, place a high—and, I would argue, exaggerated—value on cognitive capacity. . . . When [it] has been so severely diminished, the wishes of residents are given little credence. In most matters—health, romance, personal freedom—nursing homes may rank the desires of residents below the needs of the families involved and below the needs of the nursing home itself."

It's dusk: a watery-purplish, indefinable time between staff shifts. An orderly—is it an orderly?—ambles down the hall, each arm around a wobbly resident. They clearly require his steadying touch. They bump and lean against him. They nearly obscure him. And then, at the door to Daniel's room, they smile, smartly swivel around, and flee back the way they had come. Eloise removes the cap from her bunned hair, and enters his room—a final time; they know they can only manage this duplicitous switcheroo once. But they want closure to their aborted affair—closure of their own making. And his partially palsied fingers at length undo her orderly's buttons.

"People with dementia may be unable to recall past events, but in most cases they are still able to reproduce meaningful relationships, because what is called 'semantic memory' remains intact . . . what enables people to assign meaning to what they experience in the present, unrelated to their personal history.

"Although cognitive memory is compromised in dementia, it may well be that affective—or emotional—memory is not."

And so yes, they meet this once more, from out of their fog, and yet held in their fog, like spies who convene in a steam room. He forgets his pill that's sunk to the bedside tumbler's anodized bottom. She's forgotten the name of the home, she's forgotten *she's in* a home, the planet's fallen as wholly away from her as her shirt. But what they need to remember—they remember.

This, in fact, is the gesture out of which our chemicals were born. From the void, they were born—from the First Occurrence, fifteen billion years ago, in wisps of primordial universe-gas over 500 million light-years long. And gravitational forces within these supravast-but-insubstantial trails slowly shaped them into "dense clumps" that themselves, over billions of years, "evolved into all existing matter."

From out of the mists, a shape: Hello, I'm Dorothy Wordsworth, and no other. Have you seen my William about?

On the lip of a cliff-edge: Chen Shou: "I lean on my bramble staff / And gaze into space."

From out of the mists: particularized.

For this we fight, to be a single cohesive perimetered thing. And if not? — "senescence," we call it. "Transcendence," if it's desirable.

"They'll come for us soon."

"Soon. Yes: soon."

I don't know what they've been doing on this bed while I've pictured the cosmos forming. I know now, though, that they're holding each other, length against length, and saying each other's name like a charm, repeatedly, a charm against dissolving. On the table: a tumbler of cloudy water. The pill isn't there, but the pill is still there.

A TRIP TO THE COUNTRY OF DEATH, AND BACK

Current Events: A Diptych ～～

#1117

From here we can see the combination smoke as it ascends
from a field over to the east: a greasy column of fuel on fire,

and incinerated human bodies. One wing still is intact,
it angles up and shines with schizophrenic cleanliness . . .

the sirens . . . an odor of death on the wind. . . . And once
again, we're ashamed to carry the small weight

of our day's complaints to the edge of an actual tragedy.
A thimbleful of ear-bones stained by office innuendo . . .

a pebble . . . a gram of sexual jealousy . . .
we bring them to the brink of this wound in the earth,

and they're inadequate, even as tinder, even as salt.
Our language fails: "tinder," "salt," and we're ashamed

to use our metaphors in the face of this literality.
"A thimbleful." "A pebble." "In the face." Although

the marriage *did* crash. It died. It lost its way,
and it died. At night sometimes

when she lay in the bed, I know that there were thoughts
inside her skull like the voice in the black box saying

whatever they say as the flight goes down.

Some Common Terms in Latin That Are Larger Than Our Lives

From a description in a catalogue of rare science-fantasy titles: "Involves a utopian society in Atlantis, war with giant apes, prehistoric creatures, dragon-like beings, etc."

Mutant-engineered bloodsucker djinns, invisibility rays,
lost civilizations, past-life telepathic romance
—anything, finally, can fit in *etcetera,* even in
its abbreviation; much as in some story

out of Borges, where the world is the same as a library
holding all of the books in the world, and one book
holds the sentence "This is all of the books
in the world," so is, by itself, sufficient. Or

this woman on the streets of Manhattan, September 11,
2001: the look in her face is a gene
of the entire holocaustal event; fast-forward to it
any time you need to construct that whole

unbearable day. And other people are huddled
under girders, shrieking out as if to angels somewhere
at the edges of this, to presences outside of the human
—gods, and demons, and beings of the supernatural realms,

et alia. And others are too dazed even for that;
they're empty now of everything except a stare
at the incomprehensible shape of things, the sky,
and what's beyond the sky, and beyond that, *ad infinitum.*

About the Dead

The wooden leg obviously = a prosthetic leg.
The man with a seed from a tree
on his pants leg = the prosthetic sex of a tree.
The glass eye = a prosthetic eye.
And a telescope lens?—the dream life
of the glass eye when it's closed.
The car?—prosthetic speed.
To someone blind from birth
who has no way to context blindness, never having known
its opposite—silence is prosthetic blindness.

If the world's the "web of life"
my high school bio textbook employed as a phrase
to refer to a global ecosystem, *everything*
becomes the viable, artificial enablement
of something somewhere. Everything
—and everyone.

Nathan and I are discussing Keats—the late
autumnal dolor of the Odes; we're lightly
arguing, then somehow we're regluing our opinions
into a single admiration, we're reciting grand
collaborative swatches of his language
and our beer breath, and (there's this about the dead)
he's here, he's more here every minute,
almost crowing with delight now, almost dancing
between us—no, not "almost": *dancing*—
on these two crutches of his.

Swan ⁓

Not just as individuals, but also as a couple, they
were so demure . . . no, not "demure" exactly, but a sort
of gracious quietude attended them, and *then*
at the end—and everyone remembers the night of alternating
operatic solos of confession over drinks at The Italian Gardens—
something seized them, something like a sudden lyricism
so demanding of its vessels, that it used them up.
The Greeks of course said the same of the swan: its whole life,
mute; and then that single one-hour flower of fine
coloratura. What's a Geiger counter if not an ear
for how the ticking death-song of uranium echoes faintly
over time? "I heard" the speaker says in a novel of Clifford Simak's
"the tiny singing of the tiny lightbulb and I knew
by the singing that it was on the verge of burning out."

Lucky's Story

They won't be stopped. And when one stropped
a razor and they took away the razor . . . well,
he slowly choked himself to death
by swallowing the leather strop. One pushed
the wooden handle of a floor broom down
her willing throat. One did the same
with a hundred-count packet of needles.
Nothing stops them in their need to have
no further need. We lock them up, and leave
with the key, and they'll beat themselves
to a bleeding mess with the lock. One
tightened a screwdriver into a vise, and then
repeatedly threw his throat and eyes
against it. One did similarly
with the crucifix from her communion.
Nothing is cautionary enough to supersede
their drive: one woman slashed her own throat
in her ninth month, and a pastry chef
from Buenos Aires injected a dose
of a prize-winning sugar glaze into his veins,
this is true, this is representative of thousands
every day, there is no light that we can shine
which will be sovereign over what a single pinprick
of their darkness will let in. They won't
be stopped, and if we take away the lock,
and the strop, and the broom, and the sixty unstoppered jars
of leeches that a man in Marseilles slathered
simultaneously on his skin . . . even then,
bereft of their props, they will find a way
for their own tormented bodies to sour
inside of their cells more quickly than the rest of us
and, often enough, more horribly.
                                    Then is it

a surprise? or the fulfillment of a common expectation?
—that the rest of us exhibit such tenaciousness
in holding to our lives: my mother
scuffled with the Reaper over even sixteenth-inches
of the working lining left inside her otherwise
enflamed and peeling lungs. Or thirteen-month-old
Donna Anderson;* or Raphael Ledoux.** If even
one remaining molecule of hand can cling to one
remaining molecule of cliff . . . it will, and it will pull
the rest of the threatened body up to safety.

Every one of us

---

* —who had wandered out of her family's house
on a -76° night in the century's worst December, and was found
only after "her heart had been stopped
for at least 90 minutes, perhaps as long as three hours.
As they lifted her onto their operating table, doctors
heard the ice crystals cracking throughout her body."
She survived. Her system hibernated deep inside itself,
and she survived.

** —who was pinned to the earth
when north winds sent a dead tree crashing
immovably onto his left (and shattered) leg. Three
hours later, certain no one
would discover his location in those wicked timber heights
before the night chill and the mountain wolves arrived,
he went to work on himself with a pocketknife,
and a shirtsleeve for a tourniquet, and then crawled
to the logging road, where weekend campers
stumbled on him "passed out, but revivable. He is now
a happy one-legged father of two, and still goes
into the foothills exploring for Indian flints."

contributes to this balance—those who rush to exit;
those of us who fight to remain. It makes
an equilibrium—if not to someone
at the scene, and overwhelmed
by, say, that girl whose thirteen-month-old shoulders
could be raked across like ice
. . . still, there must be a counterweighting
as it's "understood" by the universe,
as it's "seen" by the "eyes" of the universe,
as it takes place in the leveling wills
of proton and electron, in the unappeasable battles
of matter and void, in the astral-and-vacuum sets
of ledger books with the parallel lists:
Departure and Resistance.

One line.
Then another line.
And another.
We do this enough, we write it and read it
enough, and we really do come to believe
that there's an order to things. And if
there's not . . . but we can't even write "there's not"
without its being a meaningful verbal structure.
Just a single letter: one free-floating A
is still a dot in a continuum
that goes back to the horned head of the Sumerian ox.
Well, whoopydoo; but surely there *is* "chaos."
Yes—and we can look it up, in its place in the dictionary.
"Manic" says that somewhere there's a great
depressive brick which waits for *its* turn on the balance-pans.
And I can bring us into a scene

in the dark knot where an alley loops around a grid of sewer pipes,
in Chicago, in the tattered end of the autumn of 1958
—a place and a time nobody ever goes to anymore,
but I was there, and I saw the man in the dirt with his chest
spread open, and there was the stark white trellis
of bone in an atrium so red, it's stained a small pinch of my mind
that shade and won't be worn away no matter how strenuously
I rub it with the intervening years.
That man . . . he'd done it to himself. But if I bring us there,
then I'm also required to tell you—in fulfillment of the laws
of the dynamics of the cosmos—that my friend's son Nelson
gingerly entered the room where his grandma Angela was failing
day by day from the leukemia, he lifted up the palm of his hand
he'd lightly struck with a paper cut, and pointed
to its smeary blood, and said, "Grandma,
here: you can have mine."
Such was the call of life, to life,
she leaned to his open palm and licked it clean.

Death sometimes travels a long long way:

for instance, the man who trained in CPR
and found his neighbor—she had always seemed
so tragically susceptible to things—on the ground:
a strangling, face-empurpling gurgle.
Sorry to say: she died, despite the efforts he bent
to her bitter lips. She died: a suicide. And sorry
to say: his contact with the cyanide overcame
the attempts of EMS to save *him* an hour later.

But this is also a verified story:

a lady named Erin—a certified nurse—
walked into her sister's trailer home
to discover that woman, nine months pregnant,
dying from a self-inflicted knife wound
to her throat. A maybe one-in-fifty chance
of ever coming-to again—if that—
if tended to immediately with Erin's emergency training
and with miraculous ambulance promptness.
That was *one* choice; Erin made the tough,
casesarian other. The knife was right there;
soon enough, in a widening puddle of blood,
so was her nephew. Then
she carried him out, a long long way
—out of that place, to someplace better.
He lived.
That was the name they gave him: Lucky.

THROUGH HISTORY ON PENNIES A DAY: 2

The Rocket Ship ⟿

He hasn't thought about it since he was twenty-five,
and—here it is! in a box, in the attic, and still shrill
in its candy red and deeply mango yellow 1950s plastic,
carefully molded into the astrodynamic silhouette
of "the future": all those "solaratomic" fins
a spaceship evidently would require in the year 2000.
Now he's fifty-five . . . and, for a minute, as he lifts it
to the window, the air of the attic really does become
the cat's-eye swirl of gases that's the atmosphere of Jupiter,
and then . . . well, *anything* then. Anything antigravity
and faster-than-light. It's based on the one, the "real" one
in the TV show, that had a "radium blaster" on its sleek nose.
This one, too: a sky blue plastic blaster the size of a toothpick.
When he'd thought of it the last time, he was with a woman

*—thirty years ago!—*and running his tongue along
the butter of her thigh when, very gently, but assuredly, she
stopped him with a single finger set against his forehead,
to explain the scar. It was, she said, a surgical scar.
She had cancer. All they could do right now was plant
a kind of "seed" (that was her term), a radiated capsule,
into her leg and hope for the best. For him of course it isn't
a seed: you know, now, his own metaphor of choice. He sees it
taking off, *fooming* through the cosmos of the body,
her body, that easily seems to be worthy of the theorizing
of Einstein and of Hawking; maybe everybody's is.
She died, by the way. There was never anything after
twenty-five for her. But he lifts her out of his memory now,
unwrapping her with something of the quiet awe he felt that night.

Time in the Victorian Novel ⟶

It takes sixteen pages simply for the heroine's
family history, from Eden
to those ill-advised investments of her father's
in an Indies cane plantation. Nineteen
pages more of antimacassars, barouches,
and barrister-wigs before we hear her name.
Another seven hundred, just to learn her mole
is in connection to the peerage.
                                    Somewhere
else, on the boardwalk, kwikee
rollerblading and razorscootering declare
the pace; my friend Deaneen did seven men
in seven nights in her beach-house rental.
Here, though, in Chapter the Eighth, Part Four . . .
a slower time; as water is
a slower space than air.

⟶

My Dearest Cousin—,

    The sun's felicitations after a long and arduous dark are no more welcome than are your greetings to me in your letter of only a fortnight ago. These now I return, with hugs enough to cover the roof of the parsonage in place of its hundreds—surely I remember hundreds?—of doves. And by those tokens, you will know how much you are missed.

    And most particularly, I miss the genuine solace you offer, Cousin, and your homiletic wisdoms, in the presence of such trials as mine. It is never easy to lose a parent; more so, when the other parent has already slipped away from the hold of this world (you will remember my father's tragic voyage to his Indies estate, to oversee the last of the cane: they tell me that the serpent was the length of three great walking-sticks). And I feel as cruelly hammered upon (by Fortune) as the stageboard of the Punch and Judy shows (by the wooden foreheads of those hand-animated worthies!)

    Even as I consider my mother about to be lowered tomorrow into her grave, and feel the upwelling sorrow in me, I also puzzle over this opaque and elusive idea of ours, "Eternity," of which the vicar spoke to us last evening on his frayed settee; and I wish I had your counsel, Cousin. My mother is out of all seasons now; it seems to me a bar of metal is more, still, in the realm of changes than she. No, she has stepped off the edge of Time, and a wonder comes over me to think of it . . .

[etc.].

⌒

Seven

One man (metaphorically) exploded
into a neat, blue-orange Bunsen-burner flame: *ssst*,
he was gone. How long is "etc."?—the crack of a whip?
—the crack of a fault line under a famous
and tectonically endangered urban center?
Etc. the length of a gene.
Etc. the route of the nineteenth-century mail coach
from London to the Uplands station.
One man she broke as easily as a dinner candle.
One, the next, reduced her to what might have been
a pliable rubber device for the night, and nothing more.
One knew a yoga trick to do in bed; but first,
a koan. How long is "a koan"?—to the clock?
—to the centralmost nub of the breath,
the orchidaceous layers of the breath?
The time of the striderbug in a tide pool.
And the time of the tide.
She'd walk the beach each afternoon and try
to be open to every understanding
—what does the man with the chest incision staples see?
—what does the sandpiper see?
—or the sand? Most days, however, she couldn't understand
her own loud, quickly ticking needs.

Was she a clock? Well, yeah: *of course*
a body's a clock. The time of the gull
and its platitudinous shrieks. The time of the pleasure
of human flesh. The time between its pleasures.
One man seemed as if . . . but she couldn't even remember.
His entire meaning happened for her in the time it simply takes
for guests to introduce themselves at a Victorian novel's
dinner party. The time of those turned pages.
The mail coach still en route. A gull's reflection
turning in a tide pool: it's the hand of a clock.
One man was a fucking animal, which was great
and then it was bad; but what was great remained
as strobe-light flashes of memory. What unit
measures memory? (There's "cubic"; why not "mnemonic" yards?)
She'd try to be open. But she was a clock,
which can't be open; a clock is a boundaried system.
The time of the knowledge of death.
The time of Sarah and Abraham. Of neon in a sign.
One man was actually a boy: at least in character,
she never really asked about his age.
But clearly . . . those lack-of-experience eyes . . . his time
was some world's other than hers, its revolution
made a different elliptical orbit around its sun.
And when she was done with them, well . . . she came home,
and that time in her life was over, used up. Time
for Chapter the Next.
The time of the pane of window glass that's thickening already
at its bottom, it's so old; it may have even been old
in the time of Thomas Hardy and of George Eliot,
at work on scenes in Victorian novels.
The time it takes a dipped quill pen.

The "Nazca lines" on the high plateaus of Peru:
marks, on a clock of the gods.

⌐⁓

I've counted. I've enjoyed each vast, discriminating
sentence—each is a mansion of many
semicolon-architected rooms.
And I know: eventually in the Victorian novel
someone drowns. I've counted, and by page 863
somebody rises suddenly (deservedly) in rank.*
Somebody's rotten marriage perishes. Sex
occurs (although *between* the chapters). Death
is occasion for much talk, and enormous words. It happens,
everything happens—although in the way
some beauties deepen, and some signs of age
become a living scrimshaw on a person's face,
when you live with that person, and really *don't* see it
happening in its graduated, day-to-day progression.
If it's seemed to be a swifter set of dramas
for Deaneen . . . at the end, the result is still
that beauty, and those lines that are the price
our faces pay for bearing beauty.
One summer, I rented a very old house in the English uplands.
It was being renovated—and so a window
that the carpentry men had just installed last week
was only three steps down the hall
from one that Trollope could have looked through,
or Dickens, or Thackeray, a window
slightly sallow by now, clouded, and thick

---

* Perhaps her mole is a sign; or perhaps
this information finally arrives by mail coach, in a trunk.

at its bottom with the infinitesimal
downward flow of glass. Three steps. And so
the view from out of each was different.
And yet, of course—the weaving row of trees,
the sky, a curl of village smoke—enough the same
to be the same.

Poet-Spouse Observer-Thoughts ⁓

1.

The saddest face I've ever seen—I mean
from no immediate occasion, just a thin and continuous
underbuzz of ill content—is Sammy Shore's, in all four
of the high school yearbooks scattered on the tables
at the 30th-year reunion of the class of 1972
of Argonia High in Argonia, Kansas: site, it seems, of hijinks
worth Homeric recitation, and home
to the dread Red Raiders. Sammy Shore's not here
this night with my wife the guru of junior college Web design
and the other Argonia High escapees (the dentist,
the trucker, the nurse on the cardiac ward: I meet them all)
and yet it's *his* whey-white and restless, skimpy shrivel-of-a-face
—so fully miserable among those halfass smiles—that acts,
at least for me, as symbol: strewn
about this beery low-key joviality.
Wherever he went and is, he's also here in the moon
whose punched-in face appears increasingly clearly in the pool
as evening gathers, and he's here in the awkward silences
between the faces of 1972 and these, their own
implausibly misshaped adult counterparts.
Our yearning for eternity . . . and the drizzle of mortality . . . for a moment they
uneasily coexist, here in the barbecue line, the way they do
in that famous gaffe from Johnny Logan, shortstop-then-sportscaster,
when he received an award: *I will perish this forever.*
—Those are poet-spouse observer-thoughts. And yet for the reunionees
it's all about the nitty-gritty catch-up: Pat,
whose daughter "has Tourette's, but not the kind where they bark
and say 'cocksucker'"; Elroy Webb, who worked the lumber store,
and then the plumbing store, and then the dry goods; Anne,
"remember Anne?" who, even though she was "happily married,"
"ran off with an undertaker."

2.

My friend L., in the hospital . . . I visit her
on the following day. Her amniotic fluid's started leaking,
and the IV feed of some thick space-age wonderwater meant
to still her premature contractions also tends to still
her lungs. It's not a good time, here amid the vased azaleas
and the standard-issue Sisters of Innocence pewter Christ on the wall,
and so I use—I really misuse—Sammy Shore for easy
levity. Once, the teacher left the room and he immediately
pulled his penis out and started masturbating—right in class.
Ensuing gasps and hubbub. Skyler couldn't see from where
she sat, and when she asked her squirming row-mate Tyler what
was happening, that shy and forthright guy could only think to say
"Well . . . Sammy Shore's let his horse out of the barn
and he's taking it for a gallop." *That's* hilarious
and sad. And so I add, by way of tempering the latter, a summation
of the moment when we left the party—earlier
than most—and I requested (well, why not?) a group performance
of the Raiders fight song. What came next
—the fight song, and the Cheer Team song, and the rest, for another
thirty heartfelt megadecibel minutes—was the evening's whole
crosstemporal experience condensed: these offkey, choral
forty-seven-year-olds morphing in and out of kids whose fists and zits
and dreams and hormones and hiked-high skirts and sheer oomphed-up raw spirits
rocked the Pep Squad bus, once—in between Argonia and East Temple County—
into a ditch. And one's not here tonight because it's noon for her
in Paris, where she's spending all the money from her chichi runway heyday
as a paparazzi favorite. One's not here because the cancer ate her
down to a single throwaway bone a decade ago already. . . .
'Bye to L., and on my way out there's that room of sweetly incubating preemies,
row on row . . . one doesn't say it to the parents, but
these bundles of joy are dice in a crapshoot
over the length of lifetimes. That night, Skyler's already asleep

when I get into bed. So still . . . I need to check, and for a second
place my fingers underneath the slow and gentle drumming of the paws
of breath that power her nocturnal engine flawlessly into the dawn.

3.

A *favorite* story: Skyler was having her hair done
in some au-courantish coif, and her beautician LaTeena
asked her, since a potentially special occasion was implied, what
she was doing that night. "Oh," Skyler said, "my husband's
giving a reading." LaTeena stopped mid-curl, a look
of sudden comprehension washing in delight
across her face. "I didn't *know*," she said, and nearly couldn't
continue from the excitement, and from the worlds that lavishly opened up
in front of her at this news, "your husband's a psychic!"

Yes I am. And I can tell you this:
We're all going to sing. We're all going to meet
in what our language used to call the gloaming,
as the stars start to appear like some extreme-dimensional
musical notation, and the fireflies
begin to smear their love-calls on the surface of the dark,
and we're going to sing then, crow and cockadoodle
and chant our fucking heads off, loud and scratchy-voiced,
and showily and shamelessly alive. We're
going to yell the hell-and-back, campaigning fight songs
of the armies of the world as well as of the territorial
jousts of krill and paramecia, we're going to give
the rousingest rendition of the cheer songs and the pep songs
of the tides of Earth and the gases of Saturn's rings,
the night is nigh, you heard me: nigh, and there's
no barbershop quartet or nasty gansta' rap beyond
our voices' striving. We're going to yodel

and hiphop and do-si-dodel, and sing our souls
like bloomed heat up a flue. We're going
to melodize and croon, to shrill our enemies' names
and lullabye our honeys'. We're going to shnoogle
and canoodle and do the hokey-pokey and eensy teensy spider
in a thrice. I tell you: we're going to sing
this human song until it's our turn to answer the door,
and straighten our clothes, and nod *yes,* and
with one last whoop, and one look back,
run off with the undertaker.

A Gesture Made in the Martian Wastes ~~~

> *Berild moved. She went inward into the ruin, slowly, carefully, and then*
> *she put out her hand as though she was touching the long-vanished wall,*
> *as though she was feeling along it for a doorway that had not been there*
> *for ages. It almost seemed to Stark as though she could see the vanished walls,*
> *and was following them.*
>
> ~ Leigh Brackett, *Eric John Stark: Outlaw of Mars*

1.

Ancient Earth's a boomboom afternoon
in the video game-room of a local mall, compared
to ancient Mars in the sci-fi novels of Leigh Brackett.
Her red planet was immeasurably old—I mean
the life there was, its science, and its loud, somewhat Moroccan,
desert fierceness—when the closest thing to human life
down here was a cowering thing in its first cave.
We were learning to coordinate our fingers,
we were first distinguishing other from self, and up
there in the marketplaces of Valkis, Jekkara,
and Barrakesh, and the other towns along the dying canals,
the barges unfreighted their wares to the gaudily saddled backs
of huge dunes lizards, and the warriors warred,
the sages were sagacious, and the dancing girls in their finery
(and out of it), in ankle bells and with their invisible,
viable hooks of floral musk, created a life
that Brackett tells us overspilled its skin
with a "wicked vitality." And yet even *this* world only thrives
by sucking on the sloughings of an earlier age of wonder
—is a small thing in the weedy debris
of the formerly glorious era of the Ramas,
when their alabaster palaces seemed to rival Mars's moons
in size and scintillance, and since-lost psycho-astral physics
meant that the elect could send their minds to live in other,
younger bodies, and so never truly die. It turns out Berild

(from my epigraph) is one of only three Ramas left alive
millennia later. In the double Martian moonlight of a knotty plot,
our hero, Stark, uncomprehendingly witnesses this svelte seductress
(elderly, really, by thousands of years) extend her hands
to feel her way among the walls and statues of a city
that no longer exists. The prose is bewitchingly eerie.
I was sixteen when I read that book: the right age, evidently,
for its fecund and escapist charm to shape me
(well, my yearnings; not my gawky, daffy actual outer being)
in its image. I was sixteen, I was yolk, and mist,
and milk, and so I daydreamed I was steel.
I was sixteen, and the thought of Berild's empress body
somehow entered my genome. Ever since,
her simple gesture there amid the desert emptiness
returns to me a few times every year in weird mimesis.
Like last night, down at The Chugger Lounge. A vet from 'Nam
was alternately staring into blottospace and telling me about
the things he'd seen—and this was real
shit-your-johnnies combat duty, not some little wipe-ass
paper-shuffling office job. Well, after one especially
unexpected rain of enemy firepower, there
was his friend, his best friend, Eddie D'Amato, feeling
gingerly over the ground with one arm
for his other arm, that had been torn off in the darkness. Only seconds
had gone by, but already he reached out into that past
of himself as if it were countless centuries.

2.

"Man!—there's lots of *me* out there"—in which I hear,
across the dreary wires of long-distance, my friend Delrae's
sadly whimsical shrug. It's six months now,
he says, since Cindy found him ("and the boys were with her:
that's the part I can't stand") in the farther unkempt tangles

of their back lot, on his knees, out by the boundary marker,
weeping. "Not for any special reason. Just . . . oh, weeping;
and unable to stop. The more that Sammy said 'Please, Daddy,
stop,' the more . . . well, you get the picture." Yes,
I get this very American, commonly grievous, senseless, diagnosis-of-bipolar
picture. "Now I spend most afternoons at the downtown library:
R and R." That's where the population of "me" comes in—the retiree guy
whose reigning fear is he might fall in the cracks between the all-too-many
hours a day holds. Plus, the shufflers. The starers. The readers
afloat on books like rafts across some dread abyss. "My brothers
and sisters. The Delraes—" then "—a dynamite name for a rock group, right?"
He's been reacquainting himself with the texts of his early undergraduate love,
prehistory. It turns out that my friend Delrae can take me from
the oldest chunk of vomit that we know of (it's an ichthyosaur's,
160 million upchuck years ago) to the ocher-and-cinnabar-bodied gods
and animal-headed shaman(?) [maybe] presences on the stone
of the Paleolithic . . . on the stone of our first duplicated awe.
"And, yowza: those goddesses. . . !"—he means the bulbous statuettes that look
as stuffed with fecundity as udders, only scored with small abrasion-faces—
". . . !" and once again my friend is wordless, struck dumb by the boyish
enthusiasms I remember roiling inside him from twenty years back. Which *is*
the point of these leisurely afternoons . . . Delrae's attempt to recover
a previous self and its web of connections. *And so Berild*
enters the poem once more. . . . Delrae reaching back to an earlier
Delrae-prime: who reaches toward a paleontologist hero of his: who
enters the cave, and stretches out his hands to trace the red
and readied spear-arm of a hunter: who, in the "real world," is staring
empathetically (and chrono-regressively) into the eyes of the grazing beasts,
the shambling beasts, the howling beasts way out in the hills: who turn
their gaze at night to the pinpoint star-show overhead in the heavens
and yowl in a reunion with the elements we were at the start:
before there was mind, before there were solids.

3.

Speaking of stars . . . in one review: "If a Goldbarth poem is a *real*
'Goldbarth poem,' you know 'the universe' is going to be brought onstage,
with the full duties of a protagonist." Well, okay; so as not to keep you
waiting: here she is. She's here, she enters in the proto-radiation
of her youngest existence—so far back, the particles of space
were just her dream life; and breath, and fire, and really anything
approaching "combination," was the craziest fancy. This is the X,
the ur-speck, that astronomers would call the "singularity"
at the origin-tick of "inflation," and what *I* call (after all,
the "every" of "everything" is waiting in here to clamber out
in wings of flame and jolts of electricity and bodies of carbon)
the pupaverse. It's this all-radiant dot that the astronomers
are attempting to reach, by following the background
of "inflationary gravitational waves" across the entire 15 billion years of time
that Time consists of. And this urge to extend
our most sensitive feelers retroward, to the birth of the stars,
then *past* the birth of the stars . . . is strong, is satellites
and ground observatory installations that by now can dwarf
the grandeur of the Babylonian ziggurats to Monopoly pieces.
Then again, the promise, the wow, is equally strong . . . that some day
these astronomers will dig their hands inside the astonishing contents of the sky
with the easy intimacy of feeling around in the golden fill
of a feed bag. As for me, at the end of a day of this
and that and talking to Delrae, it's enough to rub my eyes
—these tiny packets where a partum of the stuff of stars
has come to rest—and watch what German frankly and euphoniously
calls *eigenlicht,* in its manageable (but nonetheless
blazing) display. Now, having entered the poem
myself . . . it isn't about the cosmos anymore. It's all
about me. —Although I hope that means it's also all
about you, as I stumble from bed for another sixteen waking hours
of who-knows-what, and see for a moment, or *think* I see

for a moment . . . there . . . no, *there* . . . a fog . . . a flimmer . . . and I reach out
toward that sixteen-year-old boy from forty years ago,
who's only a hole in the air now, that the wind blows through,
the wind of Mars, in its immemorial quarrel with stone
and skin and the scurf of the planet itself
and our on-loan solar resplendence.

Space and Time

Three Days: Three Sections ～～

1.

It's a thousand years after the last real city.
Humanity is nomadic again, is scattered bands
with collapsible tents (the cherished fabric remnants
of an earlier acrylic time, an urban
and technological time, when women and men
—the Old Ones—pushed the buttons of gods,
and commanded the magic dazzle of gods,
in Nyawk, and Cawgo and Ellay: fabled places).
This is a desert world, at most a world
of dry, depleted plains, of weather
larger than any frail human encampment.
Just an empty rusted aspirin tin or coil of rubberized wire
is nearly a holy token of the Old Days: our protagonists
have never seen more physical proof of their heritage
than a standard dime-store doorknob. You
can imagine their awe when, one day, forced by drought
across new hill land, they encounter the remains
of a cloverleafed freeway. Touching it. Following it.
Surely it will lead them to the Old Ones. Surely,
if only they follow it faithfully, the legends
will come true, and their lost legacy
of speech-machines and flight-machines will be
regained. Two dozen of them, with bundles
on their heads or hip-slung, solemnly, daily,
walking along the cracked lanes. Waiting

2.

is what the book is all about: not its subject;
its *purpose.* It takes all day for the jury to be selected,
it takes two weeks for the medical guys to decipher your slide,
it takes an entire life to die, and pages require being turned
in the vast, vibrating meanwhile. MEANWHILE, little clues
arrive that hint at the presence of other and hitherto-unknown
peoples: scat in the sands, and once a rusted-shut zipper
(a *zipper!*), and mainly the ever increasing evidence that
the freeway is repaired to some extent, its jagged rifts
filled in with leveled debris, its surface swept.
Our determined protagonists (two stand out especially:
a couple in love, of course) continue on their difficult journey,
patient, and crazy with expectation. One day, at last,
they encounter the pitted body of a Cadillac
on hand-hewn wooden wheels, being pulled by a team
of half-tame dogs. They haven't encountered the Old Ones, no;
they've met the population of a large and complex cult
that has small access to the gutted-out, torn husks
of former times (the shell of a telephone, an emptied dehumidifier)
and keeps the freeway clean, and lit
along its sides at night with wavering garbage fires,
in readiness: they're sure *some* time
the Old Ones will perceive this dedication, and return
with sparking gifts, and a Millennium will begin. For now,
their chosen task is preparedness. Waiting

3.

is what this poem is about, and what it does—but then,
what *doesn't?* And if years pass, this is still its function: and
this is meant in praise of that function. YEARS PASS,
and we join our couple in what could now be called a thriving village
which exists on either side of the freeway. Dog-cars
are a busy traffic; early attempts at farmed plots are successful,
and a salt-for-leather trade with a neighboring village.
She's a priestess of the cult, and tends to the birthing and dying
of everyone in her totem-precinct (Blue Bead Totem): this
means endless political give-and-take with an intricate echelon
of Temple Bureaucrats ranked by color of bead—her days
are filled with a clay-and-stylus version of memoranda. He's
a warrior-prince, and while this sometimes means beclangored battle
with an enemy host, it normally has to do with settling
petty squabbles, taking or ignoring bribes, and holding troop inspection
while the flies hum and his superiors lacquer their nails.
One calm night they meet—their first romantic rendezvous
in many hectic weeks. They walk together into the unfarmed hills,
below the stars as huge as the lushest of temple beads, they
walk beside the freeway—remember the freeway?
Barely, she says, and she sighs. Remember the long,
lean roofless nights spent curled below its arches?
And then the redolent line of watch-fires would be lit.
The way these organized the darkness, and empassioned it.
The beauty of the waiting.

The Inner Life: A Diptych ~~~

"After

> *scraping my vertebral ledges clean of their cartilage, the doctor*
> *would insert miniature jacks, and fill the empty spaces where my*
> *discs had been with especially shaped rounds of cadaver bone."*

They may as well be as alien as body parts from Mars,
is how she thinks of it at first. And yet,
with time, they come to seem a kind
of hand-me-down, no more than that.
And yet, she wakes some nights and feels them there
as heavy as Scottish curling stones.
And yet, she sees them, rounded smooth,
with a lanolin shine. It's hard to say
they're any one thing; although we can say, can *prove,*
that they're a literal reincarnation.
The way a star can be dead, but its light still alive.
One day in her yard she cracked open a seed:
after millions of miles, its sun poured forth.

The Initial Published Discovery

In another poem, I chronicled my descent
to a level of shadow and intermittent fiery light.
It was a world of emptied faces—almost sucked out,
as if eggs the weasels got at had been turned to faces.
Wanderers and their hunched-up stalkers,
mutterers to angry private gods . . . that's who I found
down there. I was talking about
our dream life—our subconscious—but a friend said
that she thought I'd meant the New York subway system,
ha ha. Nonetheless, I give to the neurobiologists
this first identification of a mechanism, somewhere in the brain,
I call "the turnstile." It allows our passage
into the depths. And what's the morning
—what's the clear new start—if not our exiting
back into this life through the same round gate?

Washington's Ovens, Adamses' Letters　～

There are stories in which the food is so *here,*
so *immanent* . . . like the favored dish
of the emperor Vitellius, the one he named
The Shield of Minerva, the Protectress of Rome, and which
"combined such delicacies as pheasant brains,
pike livers, peacock hearts, flamingo tongues,
and lamprey milt." Of other edibles
that strike one's mind with the shuddering thud
of paratroopers, I'd suggest the rare,
expensive coffee Kopi Luwak, "beans for which
are eaten by a certain kangaroolike Sumatran animal,"
excreted, and only *then* picked, washed, and processed.
Add to that a six-foot layer cake in the shape
of a catcher's mitt, at Rick's bar mitzvah. And yet

today, instead, it's the theoretical bread
of August 19, 1781, I'm fondest over:
laboring to con the British into believing American troops
were massing in the north (in fact, his strategy would lead them
south), George Washington ordered his corps of engineers "to set
foundations toward a major camp in New Jersey so authentic that
the ovens could bake thousands of loaves of bread."
A feast!—of air. A stone complexity—of air, of pure
potential, of the wonderful nothing- and anything-space
in which the UFOs cavort like larks; and AIDS
and cancer are cured; and the well-aimed, daily, acid words
and lavish satiations of my first marriage
continue, morph, and spawn. Of ancient Rome:
"The reign of Antoninus Pius was one so undisturbed,

it almost has no history." Of course it's just this well
of zero circumstance that's richest; and we see it
in the love (and the political collaboration) of John

and Abigail Adams: "We can only know what they probably said
to each other while together, from the letters they wrote
when apart." In one, she demanded *I want some*
sentimental effusions of the heart! It's this, exactly, on display
today in the corner booth: a couple over coffee—ordinary
and uncomplicated diner coffee—whispering extraordinary things.
We can tell, by the eyes, by the way that they lean to the laws
of a private magnetism. We can tell, although we can't
hear a word. It's how we can triangulate an intimacy
from the Adamses' letters. It's almost as if
we're there as they lie down to share their sustenance.

Waters ⟿

The graduate students who studied with me
in Austin, Texas, often were gratifyingly good,
though every now and then, non-native speakers offered
a special unintentional bonbon. "What means *this:* to 'ork'
a cow"?—and he showed me the line in the book, "Some days
I hated my coworker." *That* provided delight aplenty
for my friends and myself one drowsy dusk on the patios
of The Oasis, up in the sweet, green outer-limits hills
where "everybody" went for day's-end drinks and to watch
that perfect orange-pekoe yolk of a sun break open
in touching the rim of the Earth—as if it laved
the flaming lava-orange rivulets of a blessing down the hillsides—
and we'd feel ourselves ascending giddily, lifted
by a thick bouquet of helium balloons, except
our gentle anti-gravity propulsant was so simple,
so effective, as our own beer-breath hilarity. In those days,
some days every Austin moment seemed to be afloat
in pleasure. The light released an extra charge—a depth,
an emphasis that beckoned in a sensual, chromatic way—
from both the lavish palette of greens (pecan, palmetto, oak,
and Spanish dagger) on the streets and in the parkland, *and*
from the unashamedly on-display sunned skin of the women
who graced that city. The leaves, the women . . . those were two
exuding Austin beauties that my eye was especially susceptible to,
and they were both ubiquitous, and everyone I knew then
lived an aerial inch or so above the rest of the mundane planet.
But that's only one specific kind of memory at work,
and only one specific metaphor. It's just as true
to say those were the days in which John Slatin's vision
increasingly dimmed, until he was legally blind and required
a cane. Joan Lidoff died—she was still, I think,
in her early forties—of a weak heart that ran in her family.

Of broken hearts and promises and marriages and expectations
. . . one could build a country from those scattered sherds,
if they could just be found again—the Republic of Loss.
Not all of the grief was circumstantial; some was rooted
in character, even admirable character: witness Michael's firm sense
of familial responsibility . . . and the saddle marks
it's cinched deep into his spirit. This is all the murky
stuff of images other than wings and weightlessness
. . . it's turbid, burdened, oceanbottom business;
and in fact I do remember days—entire *chains* of days—
when I'd carry my friends and their distresses around in my head
like unclean water: I'd turn, I'd hear that weighted slosh.
This week, I've visited back from fifteen years away.
"My father died last month. I hadn't expected him
to live forever; still . . . it seemed so sudden. He'd seemed so *strong*.
But after the operation, he knew. He said to me,
'They messed me up, Michael. They messed me up.'"—Michael's
eyes in telling me that are heavier than his face can hold.
They're with me now, as I'm writing this. I remember a party:
a graduate student, just arrived from Lima, Peru,
asked idly, "Whot is yor mont' ob birth?" January,
I said to her, and she whapped her forehead in recognition.
"Ah! Joo are an Aquarium!"

Problemata Aristotelis ～

1) Why does red hair turn white sooner than other hair?

2) Why does a man yawn when he sees another yawn?

3) Why is it a good custom to eat cheese after dinner?

4) Why is there such delight in the act of venery?

5) Why do birds not piss?

These and some 380 other questions, divided into 34 topical sections and complete with causal explanations, circulated widely in over one hundred editions in early modern Europe, under the title (and the vernacular equivalents) of "Problemata Aristotelis ac philosophorum medicorumque complurium."

> ～ Ann Blair, *Authorship in the Popular "Problemata Aristotelis"*

1.

The more we have, the fewer we have.
The answer, sadly enough, is "years";
and the riddle itself is the major glory and thorn
of our human existence.
                              As for "more," there was a clan
in the days of the caves—one part of a culture
spread throughout that cavey neighborhood—where every
rite of passage . . . menstruation, for example,
and the first blood drawn in a hunt, and the first
blood lost in a battle with enemies (i.e., anybody
not of the clan), and giving birth of course . . . these things
were honored with the ritual gift
of a berry red tattoo stripe, like an epaulette:
for the color of blood *is* the color of rich experience.
Simultaneously, these sequences of frequent drama
took their toll . . . the price of life is

less of it . . . and elders could be found whose skin
was entirely stippled in red dye, while
their hair had been leached, by every
further bountifulness, completely to white.

2.

Three-days-sleep away from the caves,
he became lost from the rest of the hunt,
and wandered alone on the upper ridges.
From here, when he looked down, a herd of beasts
that flashed across the plain was like a single wing,
a single eel—maybe a hundred of them
(not that "a hundred" existed yet), and they
relayed and duplicated one another's
individual rush into a synchrony.
He saw: they attracted both the kin-group hunters
of his home cave, and the hunters of another,
alien cave. One lifted a club:
another lifted a club. A spear: a spear.
He could have run to join in, but the truth
(did "truth" exist yet?) is, he fled
back to the home cave, with a tale that night
of how they'd been attacked, how he was fearless
and many enemies died beneath his blows, but
they had been outnumbered and . . . at that point
Old-one yawned: and so then Little-one yawned:
and then the whole cave.

3.

It began the way the sex act did
—the raw, fulfilling, belligerent
work of an animal, then falling asleep
immediately in a puddle of animal slobber—
and it followed the same trajectory,
it climbed its way out of the caves
until millennia later it was something
that, around the basic bestial pleasure,
had accumulated theory,
instruction, delicacy, and the gesture
of a capstone kiss as a token of completion.
And so: the meal. Eating. "Dining."
By then, it wasn't just
a fist inside a fresh kill, and
the still-contorting organs of it torn out
for our hungers; no, there was also,
now, the idea of cooking; later,
of domestication. Certain of the herd
were kept, for milk. The milk was kept
beyond a momentary guzzle, and a dozen
different richnesses of it evoked
a dozen newly felt responses from our tongue.
"Forks." "Courses." "Platters." There were ranges
of after-dinner delights. Wedge of cheddar.
Ribbons of Swiss. Soft paunch of a Brie,
sweet, musky, and ivory.
Served at the last—a capstone kiss.

4.

"Because," said Edie—and nobody ever argued
Edie's expertise in carnal arcana, she was so
. . . so *historied,* so obviously kegel-exercised—
"it brings me totally into this other self."
By which she means the self of when
we were only semi-distinguishable in the caves
from our brothers the hoofed and horned,
our sisters the fleet four-footed. We
were like them, and not
like them; we were different seeds
with the same transmission. In the dark:
the howling. In the groin: the howling.
The snuffle. The call to mix. The pull below
all thought of consequence—in fact, below
all thought, below "in fact." This was before
the formation of nicetie, and before the creation
of time; before the apple had been eaten
and the arrival of knowledge annihilated
the ignorance of bliss.

5.

She expected it, and Edie—who'd been track team
back in college once—described for her in detail
how it felt to have your body fat and even
to some extent your muscles disappear
into your marathon training. Even so,
when her periods stopped—feeding her running
with sexual fecundity itself—she felt
so rearranged, she wept . . . though later came to see
herself in her almost aerial laps
around the course as charged by superfuel.
In one dumb dinosaurs-and-cavegirls movie,
there's a special moment when the heroine
looks up from some grim, heavy Stone Age housework
at the cave mouth, and she witnesses
a leathery, feathery, cat-sized inbetweenodon
as it wriggles out of a larger predator's grip
and seems—with a squeeze of its ugly features
and a great inspired thought—to invent
the ability to fly, right then, completely: and
it soars across the screen's sky with the sudden grace
of a blocky Gothic letter becoming italicized.
We can see in her face: this woman is overcome
with the wish to evolve too. And she's learned
a lesson about its cost:
Everything—*everything*—goes into that urgent miracle.

6. through 385.

Say a journalist dies. She entered the zone
in an armored vehicle; even so, the bomb
explodes with force enough to overturn the van.
This is the risk she took, and understood
she took. But she needed to know. Her readers
needed to know. The night sky called
to Galileo—the night sky, and its punctuating
stars; just as the constellated nodules
under the skin called to da Vinci, who needed
to know, who was into it over his wrists
until his nails were packed with the yellowy
fat of the dead. With these iconic figures
on the dashboards of our brains . . . how many
eggy clouds have wafted from the vials
of amateur chemistry experiments, or bank accounts
dissolved in the quest for perpetual-motion engines?
But we need to know. It tickles
the invisible, weightless know-bone in the mind,
the way the tongue can play a spot
between the legs until it begs for more.
If it's under a scab,
then we'll pick at the scab,
we'll lift it off as cleanly
as the top half of a bagel from its lox,
or we'll chip away at it with the small unclean ferocity
of a fox claw at the weak patch in an egghouse wall
—what-, when-, how-ever, we need to know
what the pulse-pink meat of it looks like
under that tough, protective badge.
Will it hurt?
Will it hurt to strip off the layer of armor?
Listen: there's only one way to know.

I've been reading one of those frequent
"Still Unsolved Conundrums" issues so fashionable
with popular science magazines: What
is memory made of? What is sleep for?
Out of what did the universe come,
and how? Will the universe dwindle away
or implode, and I look in the mirror.
How many total species exist, and I study my face.
I hold up my hand to the afternoon light.
Will we ever define "dark matter," I worry
the this, and the that, and the where-I'm-going, and all
of the small but listable hurts I've fostered in the universe
of people whom I care about, and do they love me,
and how, and how, and how will I know.
Lucretius is *so* correct about so *many* things
(as early as *circa* 50 BC, his work explains
atomic theory, and notions central
to Newton's laws of thermodynamics) that I forgive
his mislocating the mind in the breast: and *don't* we
(some of us too often, others not nearly often enough)
think with the beats of the heart? And the heart
is greedy, as our lust to know
is greedy, it will flay the deer,
and propel itself to the moon, to Mars,
it will open the dresser drawer to see
what's hidden under the tangle of tawny chemises.
But that driving need is in the *skull*—not the chest; *that's*
where it wakes and sniffs the laden air
for pheromones of knowing. It will wear
a wig, a hood, a fake (or even real) ritual scar,
to penetrate the taboo room. It will keep
its eye at the telescope lens despite
the prohibiting edict. It will crawl

to the half-inch line of light below the shade,
and will study its neighbors caught in the rawest of postures.
It will wake—in the head, in the bowl of bone
we nurtured over millennia. It will wake
to the tang of a fresh day, and step plump with curiosity
out of its thick-walled haven, out of that cave
we come from and we carry.

WHERE THE MEMBRANE IS THINNEST

Where the Membrane Is Thinnest ~~~

1. Others

A woman is muttering candidly in her sleep; the man
beside her holds his ear against their shared air,
and . . .
           / But first we're going
into the caves—at Lascaux, Foz Côa, Saint-Cirq,
Siega Verde, Le Portel, Les Trois Frères,
and the other sites of the great dream-beasts
of the Paleolithic artists. Here,
by blind touch in these subterranean chambers,
or by reed-light, or by puddled and guttering fat-light,
here . . . the shamans, they who journey
to the Other Realms and visit with the spirits there,
are sensing where the rockface is most open
(not necessarily *physically* open, but . . . amenable,
let's say) to the recognition of underworld beings. We can see,
still—at Chauvet, and Altamira, and Le Roc aux Sorciers
and the rest—the powerful depictions that were part of this
shamanic journey to seek out the Others,
elegant ibex outlined thickly in rust reds,
an enormous lion dotted in char, the blocky bison,
and those patch-job fusions of human and animal . . .
almost, we can hear them, we can smell them, as they gather
in the throats of the cave-wall fissures . . . all of them, *almost* here,
like wild things pressing at back-porch screens
just enough to reveal themselves /
                                      . . . he hears
the names of men, of *other* men, escape and then
recede on the cyclical lift and descent of her breath,
a James, and once a Francis (man? or woman?),
this, and a wordless, purring ardor . . . and he spends the night
awake at her side, unnaturally sensitive

to any emanation from that hidden (maybe vastly
more important?) world
and its presences.

2. *"TO THE PEOPLE OF AMERICA: A SCIENTIFICK DISCOVERY!!!"*

Those nineteenth-century crackpot hollow-Earthers
don't encourage an echo of empathy
in our twenty-first-century marrow. They're too dapper
in their swallowtail coats, and too self-conscious
in their lectures at the Knights of the Trident brotherhood lodge,
and in their petitioning Congress: please, act, now,
with a federal expedition into the planet's central vault.
They're theory and mishmash Latin
under diagrams, when what we want is older
than the first root of our language, and is wearing
the freshly flayed-off skin of a stag: its antlered glory
bearing the stars in the night,
and its snout and its hooves and its wounds like mouths.

A first approach to this might be the figurines
—in clay or molded lead or wax, and found sometimes
in tiny coffins, or bound in leather strips, or pierced
with metal pins—that Roman-era professional witches
"deposited in a grave or a well or a fountain: in the realm
of ghosts or undersurface powers": where the membrane
in between the worlds is thinnest.
                                        And before that,
Theseus hunting down the nightmare half-man-half-bull
in what we would metaphorically call
"the bowels of the earth," although, in this story,
those ever-lower, ever-heavier, dark, maze-like inturnings
are given literal shape. It's only there, beyond
the light of the outer-upper world, that these two protagonists
meet.
        And so the story of Eurydice

is the tray of an old-time photographic bath
in operation. The deeper she travels,
the longer submerged: the clearer are the images
of the shades who rise to greet her.

3. Stage One

And the aurochs in its richly umber musculature
and its border the color of carbon . . . and the horse
that, in the jitter of the light, must
have looked ambient, or even roiling
out of a crack like smoke from something
boiling in the spirit world. . . . These aren't
all. There are also the abstract patterns
—zigzags, tick-tac-toeish grids, dots, nested "spoon"-curves—
that we find with undeniable consistency
amid the beasts and people shapes, across all time,
across all place: the geometric scribblework
of Africa is that of South America, is that of Europe. . . .

Clottes and Lewis-Williams say the reason is:
the caves were sites at which the shaman
entered (or commemorated entering) the trance
by which he flew to other realms; and of the three main types
of cave depiction, each conforms to one of the three successive degrees
of the trance state: so before the *second* (a whorling tunnel)
funnels the participant into the animals
and the animal-human hybrids and the phantoms of the *third* . . .
first, there's this play of vibrant and ever-flickering
diacritical shapes.
                    We see them
(or their less emphatic cousins) every day
in the shower of cold lights under our eyes' scrunched lids;
in psychedelic visions (LSD is of course an example)
and hypnotic blitzing-out; and they're still here,
as hazy memory, in the stylized crags and vortices,
the tittles and the fiddleheads,

of military insignia and jewelry design
and spray-paint wall graffiti and gang tattoos.
                                    These congeries
of hash-marks and these hills of piled circles
are a species-wide sub-language . . . up from the blood,
or even deeper than the blood . . . and every time we idly doodle
on a napkin in the corner of a bar . . . well, what we are
(and inescapably so) is latter-day, desacralized initiates
in stage one of the path of shamanic travel.

She's stopped speaking in her sleep. She's still
and cool—she's almost an architectural structure
under the bedsheet. But he knows
her mind is still a hotly oscillating ghost-domain
of history and secret. Half-asleep himself,
he gently sets his head against that other,
lower mouth . . . between her legs . . . as if
the things he seeks to know would be more likely
to collect here, and some errant wisp of information
wiffle out into the everyday world . . . and falls asleep
completely now, with his ear sealed damply against her.

4. The Most Ancient Light in Existence

And [the call / the invitation] came, to go among the wingéd ones,
and the sky opened up [disappeared] and I was among them.
And [the call] came, join the swimming ones,
and the water opened up, and I was there among the swimming ones.
And [the call] to be with the ones in the under[spaces] came,
and the stone does not open up, [the stone does not disappear],
but I watched the stone to see [its speech / its truth / its way];
and I entered the under[spaces].

～

My issue of *Time* for February 24, 2003, says
now we *know* the universe's age;
and the relative distribution of "ordinary atoms" (4%),
"dark matter" (23%), and "dark energy" (73%);
and when, in the fiery proto-origin of things,
"the first stars turned on." Now we know, because
the Wilkinson Microwave Anisotropy Probe
"a million miles from Earth" has been studying
"the most ancient light in existence," lifting its sensors
up (back? out?) to "the whisper of microwaves
left over from the Big Bang" . . . as one night the child
lifts her ear to the wall
and, on its other side, is a faint and remnant echo
of the energy that created her.

～

In issues of *Juggs* and *Leg Show* and *Coed Cuties*
are hundreds of classified ads like the one
in which Michelle (who's also Cherrie and, elsewhere, Naughty Girl)
will sell you an initial sample set
of her "sexy, wide-open pix"

for "a token of fifteen dollars." "No holes barred."
And you can typify this
in any dismissive or angered way you'd like, but
for the man I'm choosing to follow today
as he wheelchairs up to his P. O. box with trembling hands,
it's a miracle. Yes: from out of the world's impenetrable
refusals of his attentions, yes: from out of the blank
and formidable wall of postal number codes, here:
the fissure. The opening source.

5. Their Names

It's 1953, and let's face it: her life
is a mess, her life is even less than a mess,
it's "falling apart":
a man has treated her heart like a plank
in jiujitsu practice, her parents are dead
just last year in a subway wreck (the mother
six months pregnant with *her* accidental, late-in-life
"good news"), and her job. . . !—publicity
for a pharmaceutical research lab,
so every day she's torn between the jerkheads
over in science and the other jerkheads over in design,
and she *tries* to "keep up" with the news releases
out of the various -ologies, the way she tries
for her mind to keep up with Gibbon's
The Decline and Fall of the Roman Empire stockily squatting there
on her bedside desk with a stern, canonical air,
and the way she tries for her legs to keep up
with the rise and fall of the hem. It's all "too much,"
her friend Denise just bought herself one of those new
"electric mixers" (or "blender" maybe?)
in turquoise blue, and that's, *that's,* what the hokey-pokey dance
of a day can do to her! But it isn't only
dailiness that scatters her chaotically to the winds.
Is there a "God"? A . . . "purpose"? "Meaning"? Like,
take suffering: does suffering have "meaning"?
Is the world itself about to break in two,
as the euphoria of her post-World-War-II teenage years
becomes the war of "freedom versus Communism"
that's going to fill her twenties and beyond with spy planes,
fallout shelters, and federal witch hunts?
What about "love"? Hey, what about "faith"? When she was eight,

her parents took her by train on a trip out west: she still
recalls, and vividly, a wolf she saw in silhouette
on the rim of a ridge in Wyoming, saw and *heard,*
as it tilted its throat to the moon and asked the sky
a series of questions so intense, they sent the very essence
of that animal's heart out into the chilly
lacunae between the stars. It was a scholar of kaballah,
it howled so imploringly for its answers.
When the news was announced in the April issue of *Nature,*
she cried. She remembers: she read it standing
at the water cooler, casually, not really looking
for anything of a special importance, just passing the time
of her five-minute midday break, and then suddenly
weeping out loud. She'd understood *immediately.*
James Watson and Francis Crick had discovered
the shape of the structure of DNA. The shape!—do you see?
There *is* a shape, there *is* an organizational pattern
anchoring us, despite the overwhelming flux of this-and-thatness:
anchoring us, *explaining* us, there *is* a field
of neuropatterns she can conjure up now
from the deepness of the body's own unknown, unlit, unvisitable
layers, and commune with something stabler and greater
than any one life. *Of course* she weeps! *Of course* this changes
everything! Years later, in fact, a lover will tell her
(almost it seems in jealousy) that she'd even
call out their names in her sleep.

6. Art

When I look at these reproductions of tailed mages
and the herds that seem to roar like auburn storms
across the walls of the caves . . . that is, when I look
at the populace that lives below the stone
and can be seen (in certain places and under certain conditions)
through the stone, and sometimes even approaching us
as if the stone were a crossable border . . . I think
of those well-known half-completed statues of Michelangelo's,
the ones where the original block he worked
is like a womb, and the roughly indicated figure is struggling,
some of it not defined yet from its original mineral hold,
but some of it just emerged into the world of the air,
arising from a stone dream, with the stone-dust
in the corners of its eyes, and a word . . . a first word,
from the language of stone . . . about to turn
(yet never will turn) into a word of breath.

In Elihu Vedder's oil-on-canvas *The Questioner of the Sphinx*
from 1863, that monumental head is pictured
upright on the sand, in a desert
as alien and inscrutable as a moonscape.
You heard me: the head of the Sphinx.
It must be sixteen feet in height,
and solid inside with the wisdoms of the Illuminati
—formulae and covenants
that were already old when the Druids first invented
their blue dyes, and when the Zoroastrian priests
regarded the heavens from their parapets.

Knowledge like that . . . *one syllable* of knowledge like that,
if it were released—! A man is kneeling;
his ear is exactly level with the mouth of the Sphinx,
and pressed to those rose-granite lips.

Albert Goldbarth is the author of over twenty volumes of poetry, most recently *Combinations of the Universe* and *Saving Lives;* four books of essays, including *Many Circles: New and Selected Essays* (which received the annual PEN Center West Award), and one novel, *Pieces of Payne.* He is the recipient of three fellowships from the National Endowment for the Arts, a Guggenheim fellowship, and, twice, the National Book Critics Circle Award in poetry. When not budget-traveling through space and time, his home base is Wichita, Kansas.

Budget Travel through Space and Time has been set in Adobe Garamond, a typeface drawn by Robert Slimbach and based on type cut by Claude Garamond in the sixteenth century. Book design by Wendy Holdman. Composition by Stanton Publication Services, Inc. Manufactured by Friesens on acid-free paper.